IMPORTANT Inventions & Events

From the annals of 1930 Forward

Ron Berger

A handbook for those not willing to look up important events

Inventions & Events

Published by:
berger publishing
Manteca, CA 95336
mail@ronberger.com
http://www.ronberger.com

All material is copyrighted (2014) but this book may be reproduced, stored or transcribed by any means, without the express consent of the author as long as the book and author are mentioned.

Printed in the USA
978-0-9852933-4-5
First Printing
Library of Congress Control Number
2014908894

Many thanks go to Google, Wikipedia, History.com and several other sites for all their help in gathering and explaining the subject matter. This book is to help those that don't want to "look up" vital information, but want to look smart at parties. I don't pretend to have written any of the facts. Without Google and other sites there wouldn't be any book.

Inventions & Events

Ron's Other Books

The House That Ron Built

Are You Being Served Yet?

P-NUT - The Love of a Dog

"Normal" MAYDAY

Growing Old is a FULL-TIME JOB

Time for TEA

Time for More TEA

Time for Still More TEA

One Candle at a Time

The REAL Change

LOOking @ Things in General

I'll Weep for You

Back to Basics

Dear Heavenly Father

Beware of False Idols

My Minneiska

CONTENTS

FORWARD	5
1930 -1939 - Inventions & Events	7
1940 -1949 - Inventions & Events	25
1950 -1959 - Inventions & Events	51
1960 -1969 - Inventions	79
1960 -1969 - Events	91
1970 -1979 - Inventions	145
1970 -1979 - Events	157
1980 -1989 - Inventions	183
1980 -1989 - Events	199
1990 -1999 - Inventions	227
1990 -1999 - Events	235
2000 -2008 - Inventions	273
2000 -2008 - Events	279
THE END	307

Forward

"The world is very different now. For man holds in his mortal hands the power to abolish all forms of human poverty and all forms of human life. And yet the same revolutionary beliefs for which our forebears fought are still at issue around the globe-the belief that the rights of man come not from the generosity of the state but from the hand of God.

We dare not forget today that we are the heirs of that first revolution. Let the word go forth from this time and place, to friend and foe alike, that the torch has been passed to a new generation of Americans--born in this century, tempered by war, disciplined by a hard and bitter peace, proud of our ancient heritage--and unwilling to witness or permit the slow undoing of those human rights to which this nation has always been committed, and to which we are committed today at home and around the world."

John F. Kennedy spoke these words on January 20, 1961

The world is also very different today than it was in 1961. "Progress" seems to be moving at lightning speed and we find it hard to keep up. It used to be that what you bought stayed "new" for several years. Now, it is out of date before you get it home or, at the least, before you pay for it.

I thought it would be interesting to show how fast things are moving just in my lifetime. I believe I have survived and thrived in the fast growing pace that surrounds us today. I know, starting out it didn't seem like things were moving very fast. World War 2 seemed to change all that.

Of course, after that, we all breathed a sigh of relief and felt like there just couldn't be another. We all were wrong. Korea became our undoing and our thoughts of everlasting peace were shattered.

Wars seemed to have the power to push us ahead in developing new and better things. It's just too bad that so many have to die so that the remaining may live better.

Soup Lines - Starting in 1929

1930-1939-Inventions & Events.

1930:

Frank Whittle patents the first jet engine
- It's interesting to note that it took until late in 1944 before it was put to good use. Both Germany and England had a jet plane. Only Germany flew it in WW-2

The first world cup of soccer is played
- Wow - but who cares?

Polystyrene is invented
- Polystyrene (PS) /ˌpɒliˈstaɪriːn/ is a synthetic aromatic polymer made from the monomer styrene, a liquid petrochemical. Polystyrene can be rigid or foamed. General purpose polystyrene is clear, hard and brittle. It is a very inexpensive resin per unit weight.

Planet discovered (Pluto)
- It was there all along

Ellen Church, a nurse, becomes the first airplane stewardess (for Boeing)
- All stewardess had to be nurses. I don't know why. If the plane crashed the need for a nurse probably wouldn't be needed. Maybe it was to help those that had sir sickness.

1931:

Japan invades Manchuria

- This is truly the start of WW-2. The war was going on for 10 years before we became involved.

Kurt Godel publishes its incompleteness theorem
- Gödel's incompleteness theorems are two theorems of mathematical logic that establish inherent limitations of all but the most trivial axiomatic systems capable of doing arithmetic.

1932:

The first synthetic rubber is invented ("neoprene")
- Neoprene or polychloroprene is a family of synthetic rubbers that are produced by polymerization of chloroprene.[1] Neoprene exhibits good chemical stability, and maintains flexibility over a wide temperature range. It is used in a wide variety of applications, such as laptop sleeves, orthopedic braces (wrist, knee, etc.), electrical insulation, liquid and sheet applied elastomeric membranes or flashings, and automotive fan belts

1933:

FM radio broadcasting is born (Edwin Armstrong)

- Edwin Howard Armstrong (December 18, 1890 – January 31, 1954) was an American electrical engineer and inventor. He has been called "the most prolific and influential inventor in radio history". He invented the regenerative circuit while he was an undergraduate and patented it in 1914, followed by the super-regenerative circuit in 1922, and the superheterodyne receiver in 1918. Armstrong was also the inventor of modern frequency modulation (FM) radio transmission.

Unemployment in the US peaks at 25%

- One quarter of the workers in the US were still unemployed. The big downfall was in October, 1929. Roosevelt repeatedly blamed Hoover for the Depression and worsening economy. With unemployment above 20% in 1932 alone, Hoover was remiss to defend his record, and Roosevelt promised recovery with a New Deal for the American people. Roosevelt's programs never really kicked in until 1938.

Hitler wins the elections and seizes power
- Hitler didn't necessarily win an honest vote. He made it so the Reichstag "believed" he would be the "one" to make a change by setting the building on fire and blaming the communists. He gave them HOPE and CHANGE and they fell for it.

1934:

Philo Farnsworth invents the television
- We got our first set in 1953. We had to have to tall antenna and could only get two stations pretty clear and maybe sound only on several more.

Stalin's great purges: thousands disappear or are deported to Siberia
- I didn't know about Stalin until after the war. However, history has put him in the dubious spot of being number one in killing his own people.

Inventions & Events

Invention of the radar
- This may have been the most important invention of this decade. England led the way with radar and it saved the country in the "Battle of Britton".

1935:

The miner Aleksej Stakanov becomes a Soviet hero for his amazing productivity
- On the night of August 31, 1935, it was reported that Stakhanov had mined a record 102 tons of coal in less than six hours (14 times his quota). This sparked the so-called Stakhanovite movement, encouraging the rise of worker productivity.
- Stakhanov was hailed as a pioneer of innovative working methods and a role model for millions. He turned into a key player in a massive propaganda campaign to motivate workers. Urged to emulate his heroic example, plants and factories competed fiercely to outdo each other, while the man himself even appeared on the cover of Time magazine. Stakhanov and other "model workers" were promoted in the press, literature

and film. Special Stakhanovite training schools sprang up.

Wallace Carothers invents nylon, the first totally synthetic fiber

- Another great invention in the 1930's. Nylon is a thermoplastic, silky material, first used commercially in a nylon-bristled toothbrush (1938), followed more famously by women's stockings.

Ladislo Biro` invents the ballpoint pen

- Originally conceived and developed as a cleaner and reliable alternative to quill and fountain pens, ballpoint pens are now the dominant writing instrument.

Carl Magee invents the parking meter

- The world's first parking meter, known as Park-O-Meter No. 1, is installed on the southeast corner of what was then First Street and Robinson Avenue in Oklahoma City, Oklahoma on this day in 1935.

1936:

Heinrich Focke flies the first helicopter

- Henrich Focke (8 October 1890 – 25 February 1979) was a German aviation pioneer from Bremen and also a co-founder of the Focke-Wulf company.
- He is known for having developed of the turbo shaft propulsion system currently utilized by the majority of all the world's helicopters.

Economic ideas of John Maynard Keynes are applied in the U.S.

- John Maynard Keynes, 1st Baron Keynes, CB, FBA (/ˈkeɪnz/ kaynz; 5 June 1883 – 21 April 1946) was a British economist whose ideas have fundamentally affected the theory and practice of modern macroeconomics, and informed the economic policies of governments. He built on and greatly refined earlier work on the causes of business cycles, and is widely considered to be one of the founders of modern macroeconomics and the most influential economist of the 20th century. His ideas are the basis for the school of thought known as Keynesian economics, and its various offshoots.

Civil war erupts in Spain
- The Spanish Civil War (1936–1939) broke out with a military uprising in Morocco on July 17, triggered by events in Madrid. Within days, Spain was divided in two: a "Republican" or "Loyalist" Spain consisting of the Second Spanish Republic (within which were pockets of revolutionary anarchism and Trotskyism), and a "Nationalist" Spain under the insurgent generals, and, eventually, under the leadership of General Francisco Franco.

Italy invades Ethiopia, a member of the League of Nations
- The aim of invading Ethiopia was to boost Italian national prestige, which was wounded by Ethiopia's defeat of Italian forces at the Battle of Adowa in the nineteenth century (1896), which saved Ethiopia from Italian colonization. Another justification for the attack was an incident during December 1934, between Italian and Abyssinian troops at the Wal-Wal Oasis on the border between Abyssinian Somaliland, where 200 sol-

diers lost their lives. Both parties were exonerated in the incident, much to the disgust of Mussolini, as he felt Abyssinia should have been held accountable for the incident. This was used as a rationale to invade Abyssinia. Mussolini saw it as an opportunity to provide land for unemployed Italians and and also acquire more mineral resources to fight off the effects of the Great Depression.

1937:

The first nylon stockings appear
- Took awhile, didn't it?

Turing publishes his article on the Turing machine
- The "Turing" machine was invented by Alan Turing who called it an "a-machine" (automatic machine). The Turing machine is not intended as practical computing technology, but rather as a hypothetical device representing a computing machine. Turing machines help computer scientists understand the limits of mechanical computation.

Stalin's Red Terror
- The Red Terror in Soviet Russia refers to a campaign of mass killings, torture, and systematic oppression conducted by the Bolsheviks after seizing power in Petrograd and Moscow.

Rape of Nanking by the Japanese (42.000 Chinese dead)
- The Nanking Massacre, also known as the Rape of Nanking, was an episode of mass murder and mass rape committed by Japanese troops against Nanking.

Zeppelin explodes in New Jersey and ends the zeppelin industry
- The Hindenburg disaster took place on Thursday, May 6, 1937, as the German passenger airship LZ 129 Hindenburg caught fire and was destroyed during its attempt to dock with its mooring mast at the Lakehurst Naval Air Station, which is located adjacent to the borough of Lakehurst, New Jersey. Of the 97 people on board (36 passengers and 61 crewmen), there were 35 fatalities. There was also one death of a ground crewman.

Ron Berger is born
- May not be newsworthy, but here I am!

1938:

Oil struck in Kuwait, but all Arab countries supply only 5% of the world's oil
- On February 22nd, 1938, oil was discovered in the Burgan field of Kuwait. The Kuwait desert had long stood witness to several strange black patches of a rough bituminous substance; but it was not until the matter was investigated in 1935 did it become apparent that the wealth of Kuwait had remained underground for years, and was yet to be discovered.

Thousands of Jewish shops are attacked by nazi mobs in Berlin ("Kristallnacht")
- Hitler's Jew cleansing program

Hitler annexes Austria
- In early 1938, Austrian Nazis conspired for the second time in four years to seize the Austrian government by force and unite their nation with Nazi Germany. Austrian Chancellor Kurt von Schuschnigg, learning of the conspiracy,

met with Nazi leader Adolf Hitler in the hopes of reasserting his country's independence but was instead bullied into naming several top Austrian Nazis to his cabinet. On March 9, Schuschnigg called a national vote to resolve the question of Anschluss, or "annexation," once and for all. Before the plebiscite could take place, however, Schuschnigg gave in to pressure from Hitler and resigned on March 11. In his resignation address, under coercion from the Nazis, he pleaded with Austrian forces not to resist a German "advance" into the country.

1939:

First commercial helicopter

- The Bell Model 30 was the prototype for the first commercial helicopter, and the first helicopter built by Bell Aircraft Company. Designed by Arthur M. Young, the type served as a demonstration test bed for the successful Model 47.

The pesticide DDT is introduced
- First synthesized in 1874, DDT's insecticidal action was discovered by the Swiss chemist Paul Hermann Müller in 1939. It was then used in the second half of World War II to control malaria and typhus among civilians and troops. After the war, DDT was made available for use as an agricultural insecticide and its production and use duly increased.[

Flight by a jet airplane (Germany)
- The Heinkel He 178 was the world's first aircraft to fly under turbojet power, and the first practical jet aircraft. It was a private venture by the German Heinkel company in accordance with director Ernst Heinkel's emphasis on developing technology for high-speed flight and first flew on 27 August 1939, piloted by Erich Warsitz. This had been preceded by a short hop three days earlier.

Television debuts at a fair
- RCA introduced television to the American public at the 1939 World's Fair. Before the fair, they published a brochure for their dealers to explain television. The opening ceremony and

events at the fair were televised, and NBC began regularly scheduled broadcasts.

Franco wins the civil war in Spain after 600.000 people died
Hitler invades Czechoslovakia
Non-aggression pact between Hitler and Stalin
Hitler invades Poland
Stalin invades Finland
Mussolini invades Albania

- All the remaining events have to do with the Second World War. Please take a look at how this escalated into the killing of <u>50 MILLION people.</u>

The 30's were rather slow. Millions of people out of work and war looming on the horizon. The inventions that were developed couldn't be put to use immediately. Example: Television was really expensive to buy and there were very limited viewing options - like almost none.

Most of the progress to be made on utilizing these inventions were put on hold for the general population, but intensified for the military.

Inventions & Events

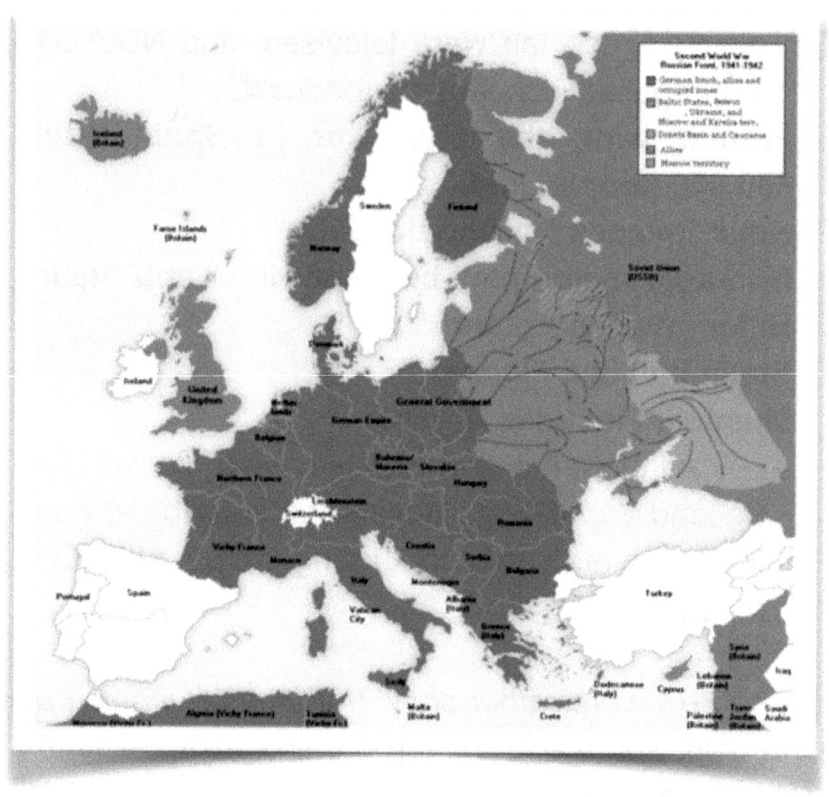

Germany's control during the War

Although the domestic landscape was getting better in the late 1939 and into 1940 it was primarily due to the acceleration of war materials that would be needed to supply our allies, hoping that we wouldn't be entering the war.

Of course that was foolish thinking, but at least we had a two year jump on getting ready.

Inventions & Events

FDR - '32 - '45   HST - '45 - '52

1940 - 1949 - Inventions & Events

1940

Battle of Britain
- In the summer and fall of 1940, German and British air forces clashed in the skies over the United Kingdom, locked in the largest sustained bombing campaign to that date. A significant turning point of World War II, the Battle of Britain ended when Germany's Luftwaffe failed to gain air superiority over the Royal Air Force despite months of targeting Britain's air bases, military posts and, ultimately, its civilian popula-

tion. Britain's decisive victory saved the country from a ground invasion and possible occupation by German forces while proving that air power alone could be used to win a major battle.

Leon Trotsky Assassinated
- Exiled Russian revolutionary Leon Trotsky is fatally wounded by an ice-ax-wielding assassin at his compound outside Mexico City. The killer--Ramón Mercader--was a Spanish communist and probable agent of Soviet leader Joseph Stalin. Trotsky died from his wounds the next day.

Nylons on the Market
- Finally

Stone Age Cave Paintings Found in France
- Cave paintings have been found all over Europe but particularly in France and Spain and the Lascaux paintings are more advanced because they are thought to belong to a later culture of the Paleolithic known as the Magdalenian.

1941:

Japanese Attack Pearl Harbor

- Just before 8 a.m. on December 7, 1941, hundreds of Japanese fighter planes attacked the American naval base at Pearl Harbor near Honolulu, Hawaii. The barrage lasted just two hours, but it was devastating: The Japanese managed to destroy nearly 20 American naval vessels, including eight enormous battleships, and almost 200 airplanes. More than 2,000 Americans soldiers and sailors died in the attack, and another 1,000 were wounded. The day after the assault, President Franklin D. Roosevelt asked Congress to declare war on Japan; Congress approved his declaration with just one dissenting vote. Three days later, Japanese allies Germany and Italy also declared war on the United States, and again Congress reciprocated. More than two years into the conflict, America had finally joined World War II.

Jeep Invented

- During World War I, the U.S. Army needed a fast, lightweight all-terrain vehicle. In 1940, the Army called on the automotive companies to create a working prototype (fitting army specifications) in forty-nine days. Willy's Truck Company was the first company to create the right prototype. The new vehicle was nicknamed "the Jeep." General Dwight D. Eisenhower said that

America could not have won World War II without it.

Mt Rushmore Completed
- The southeastern face of Mount Rushmore in South Dakota's Black Hills National Forest is the site of four gigantic carved sculptures depicting the faces of U.S. Presidents George Washington, Thomas Jefferson, Abraham Lincoln and Theodore Roosevelt. Led by the sculptor Gutzon Borglum, work on the project began in 1927 and was finally completed in 1941.

Rudolf Hess Flies to Britain on a Peace Mission
- In May 1941, Rudolf Hess, Hitler's Deputy, fled Nazi Germany. The sudden appearance of Hess in Scotland baffled many. Hitler immediately announced that Hess had gone mad and had betrayed him when he was informed of his deputy leader's flight and immediate imprisonment.

Siege of Leningrad
- The Siege of Leningrad, also known as the Leningrad Blockade was a prolonged military operation undertaken by the German Army Group North against Leningrad—historically and

currently known as Saint Petersburg—in the Eastern Front theatre of World War II. The siege started on 8 September 1941, when the last road to the city was severed. Although the Soviets managed to open a narrow land corridor to the city on 18 January 1943, the siege was finally lifted on 27 January 1944, 872 days after it began. It was one of the longest and most destructive sieges in history and overwhelmingly the most costly in terms of casualties.[

1942:

Anne Frank Goes Into Hiding

- A young Jewish girl named Anne Frank (1929-1945), her parents and older sister moved to the Netherlands from Germany after Adolf Hilter and the Nazis came to power there in 1933 and made life increasingly difficult for Jews. In 1942, Frank and her family went into hiding in a secret apartment behind her father's business in German-occupied Amsterdam. The Franks were discovered in 1944 and sent to concentration camps; only Anne's father survived. Anne Frank's diary of her family's time in hiding, first published in 1947, has been translated into almost 70 languages and is one of the most widely read accounts of the Holocaust.

The Bataan Death March
- After the April 9, 1942, U.S. surrender of the Bataan Peninsula on the main Philippine island of Luzon to the Japanese during World War II (1939-45), the approximately 75,000 Filipino and American troops on Bataan were forced to make an arduous 65-mile march to prison camps. The marchers made the trek in intense heat and were subjected to harsh treatment by Japanese guards. Thousands perished in what became known as the Bataan Death March.

Battle of Midway
- Six months after the attack on Pearl Harbor, the United States defeated Japan in one of the most decisive naval battles of World War II. Thanks in part to major advances in code breaking, the United States was able to preempt and counter Japan's planned ambush of its few remaining aircraft carriers, inflicting permanent damage on the Japanese Navy. An important turning point in the Pacific campaign, the victory allowed the United States and its allies to move into an offensive position.

Battle of Stalingrad
- The Battle of Stalingrad (July 17, 1942-Feb. 2, 1943), was the successful Soviet defense of the city of Stalingrad (now Volgograd) in the

U.S.S.R. during World War II. Russians consider it to be the greatest battle of their Great Patriotic War, and most historians consider it to be the greatest battle of the entire conflict. It stopped the German advance into the Soviet Union and marked the turning of the tide of war in favor of the Allies. The Battle of Stalingrad was one of the bloodiest battles in history, with combined military and civilian casualties of nearly 2 million.

Japanese-Americans Held in Camps
- Over 127,000 United States citizens were imprisoned during World War II. Their crime? Being of Japanese ancestry.

Manhattan Project Begins
- Scientists ALBERT EINSTEIN, who fled Nazi persecution, and ENRICO FERMI, who escaped Fascist Italy, were now living in the United States. They agreed that the President must be informed of the dangers of atomic technology in the hands of the Axis powers. Fermi traveled to Washington in March to express his concerns on government officials. But few shared his uneasiness.
- Einstein penned a letter to President Roosevelt urging the development of an atomic research program later that year. Roosevelt saw neither

the necessity nor the utility for such a project, but agreed to proceed slowly. In late 1941, the American effort to design and build an ATOMIC BOMB received its code name — the MANHATTAN PROJECT.

Atomic test
- Leaving nothing to chance, Los Alamos atomic scientists conducted a pre-test test in May 1945 to check the monitoring instruments. A 100-ton bomb was exploded some 800 yards from the Trinity site where Gadget would be detonated a few weeks later.

Nazis Raze Town in Retaliation for Reinhard Heydrich's Death
- Heydrich was attacked in Prague on 27 May 1942 by a British-trained team of Czech and Slovak soldiers who had been sent by the Czechoslovak government-in-exile to kill him in Operation Anthropoid. He died from his injuries a week later. Intelligence falsely linked the assassins to the villages of Lidice and Ležáky. Lidice was razed to the ground; all men and boys over the age of 16 were murdered, and all but a handful of its women and children were deported and killed in Nazi concentration camps.

T-shirt Introduced
- The dubbed "T-shirt" surfaced in the United States when they were issued by the U.S. Navy sometime around the Spanish American War. They featured crew-necks and short sleeves and were meant to be worn as underwear beneath the uniform. Soon it was adopted by the Army as part of the standard issue ensemble given to recruits. It got its iconic name from its shape resembling the letter "T". Dockworkers, farmers, miners, and construction type workers also adopted the T-shirt preferring the lightweight fabric in hotter weather conditions.

1943

French Resistance Leader Jean Moulin Killed
- Jean Moulin (20 June 1899 – 8 July 1943) was a high-profile member of the French Resistance during World War II.[1] He is remembered today as an emblem of the Resistance, owing mainly to his role in unifying the French resistance under de Gaulle and his courage and death at the hands of the Gestapo.

Grave of Katyn Forest Massacre Found
- The government of Nazi Germany announced the discovery of mass graves in the Katyn Forest in 1943. When the London-based Polish

government-in-exile asked for an investigation by the International Red Cross, Stalin immediately severed diplomatic relations with it. The Soviet Union claimed the victims had been murdered by the Nazis, and continued to deny responsibility for the massacres until 1990, when it officially acknowledged and condemned the perpetration of the killings by the NKVD, as well as the subsequent cover-up by the Soviet government.Italy Joins the Allies

Warsaw Ghetto Uprising

- From April 19 to May 16, 1943, during World War II (1939-45), residents of the Jewish ghetto in Nazi-occupied Warsaw, Poland, staged an armed revolt against deportations to extermination camps. The Warsaw ghetto uprising inspired other revolts in extermination camps and ghettos throughout German-occupied Eastern Europe.

1944

Ballpoint Pens Go On Sale

- It took nine years from the time of invention until they went on sale. A ballpoint pen is a writing instrument which dispenses a viscous ink from an internal reservoir through the rolling action of a metal ball at its point. This "ball point" may vary in diameter, and may be made of brass, steel, or tungsten carbide.

D-Day
- During World War II (1939-1945), the Battle of Normandy, which lasted from June 1944 to August 1944, resulted in the Allied liberation of Western Europe from Nazi Germany's control. Codenamed Operation Overlord, the battle began on June 6, 1944, also known as D-Day, when some 156,000 American, British and Canadian forces landed on five beaches along a 50-mile stretch of the heavily fortified coast of France's Normandy region. The invasion was one of the largest amphibious military assaults in history and required extensive planning.

First German V1 and V2 Rockets Fired
- The V weapons – the V1 and V2 – were used towards the end of World War Two with such an effect that the attacks on London became known as the second Blitz. The success of D-Day had speeded up the production of the V weapons and the first V1 was launched on June 13th, just one week after the Allied landings at Normandy.

Hitler Escapes Assassination Attempt
- On this day, July 20, 1944, Hitler cheats death as a bomb planted in a briefcase goes off, but fails to kill him.

Battle of the Bulge
- In December 1944, Adolph Hitler attempted to split the Allied armies in northwest Europe by means of a surprise blitzkrieg thrust through the Ardennes to Antwerp. Caught off-guard, American units fought desperate battles to stem the German advance at St.-Vith, Elsenborn Ridge, Houffalize and Bastogne. As the Germans drove deeper into the Ardennes in an attempt to secure vital bridgeheads, the Allied line took on the appearance of a large bulge, giving rise to the battle's name. Lieutenant General George S. Patton's successful maneuvering of the Third Army to Bastogne proved vital to the Allied defense, leading to the neutralization of the German counteroffensive despite heavy casualties.

1945

FDR Dies
- On a clear spring day at his Warm Springs, Georgia, retreat, Roosevelt sat in the living room with Lucy Mercer (with whom he had resumed an extramarital affair), two cousins and

his dog Fala, while the artist Elizabeth Shoumatoff painted his portrait. According to presidential biographer Doris Kearns Goodwin, it was about 1 p.m. that the president suddenly complained of a terrific pain in the back of my head and collapsed unconscious. One of the women summoned a doctor, who immediately recognized the symptoms of a massive cerebral hemorrhage and gave the president a shot of adrenaline into the heart in a vain attempt to revive him. Mercer and Shoumatoff quickly left the house, expecting FDR's family to arrive as soon as word got out. Another doctor phoned first lady Eleanor Roosevelt in Washington D.C., informing her that FDR had fainted. She told the doctor she would travel to Georgia that evening after a scheduled speaking engagement. By 3:30 p.m., though, doctors in Warm Springs had pronounced the president dead.

First Computer Built (ENIAC)

- ENIAC (/ˈini.æk/ or /ˈɛni.æk/; Electronic Numerical Integrator And Computer) was the first electronic general-purpose computer. It was Turing-complete, digital, and capable of being reprogrammed to solve "a large class of numerical problems"

Inventions & Events

Hitler Commits Suicide
- On April 30, 1945, holed up in a bunker under his headquarters in Berlin, Adolf Hitler commits suicide by swallowing a cyanide capsule and shooting himself in the head. Soon after, Germany unconditionally surrendered to the Allied forces, ending Hitler's dreams of a "1,000-year" Reich.

Germans Surrender
- On May 7, 1945, the German High Command, in the person of General Alfred Jodl, signs the unconditional surrender of all German forces, East and West, at Reims, in northwestern France.

Microwave Oven Invented
- Percy Spencer, a leading researcher of American radar technology, who would invent the microwave oven shortly after the war and its development by the Raytheon company is well documented.

Slinky Toy Hits Shelves
- In 1943, the idea for the Slinky toy originated when engineer Richard James dropped a tension spring on the ground and saw how it moved. Thinking he might be on to something a bit more fun and universal than a tension spring,

he took the spring home to his wife, Betty, and the two of them tried to come up with a name for this potential toy. After searching and searching, Betty found the word "slinky" in the dictionary which meant sinuous and stealthy. The first Slinky toys were sold in 1945 at Gimbel's Department Store in Philadelphia, Pennsylvania. And since then, stairs have never been left alone.

United Nations Founded

- On August 8, 1945 President Harry S. Truman signed the United Nations Charter and the United States becomes the first nation to complete the ratification process and join the new international organization. Although hopes were high at the time that the United Nations would serve as an arbiter of international disputes, the organization also served as the scene for some memorable Cold War clashes.

U.S. Drops Atomic Bombs on Hiroshima and Nagasaki

- On August 6, 1945, the United States used a massive, atomic weapon against Hiroshima, Japan. This atomic bomb, the equivalent of 20,000 tons of TNT, flattened the city, killing tens of thousands of civilians. While Japan was still trying to comprehend this devastation three days later, the United States struck again, this time, on Nagasaki.

1946

Bikinis Introduced
- On July 5, 1946, French designer Louis Reard unveils a daring two-piece swimsuit at the Piscine Molitor, a popular swimming pool in Paris. Parisian showgirl Micheline Bernardini modeled the new fashion, which Reard dubbed "bikini," inspired by a news-making U.S. atomic test that took place off the Bikini Atoll in the Pacific Ocean earlier that week.

Dr. Spock's The Common Book of Baby and Child Care Is Published
- Dr. Benjamin Spock's revolutionary book about how to raise children was first published on July 14, 1946. The book, The Common Book of Baby and Child Care, has become one of the best-selling non-fiction books of all time.

Juan Perón Becomes President of Argentina
- In 1943, as an army officer, he joined a military coup against Argentina's ineffectual civilian government. Appointed secretary of labor, his influence grew and in 1944 he also became vice president and minister of war. In Oc-

tober 1945, Peron was ousted from his positions by a coup of constitutionally minded civilians and officers and imprisoned, but appeals from workers and his charismatic mistress, Eva Duarte, soon forced his release. The night of his release, October 17, he addressed a crowd of some 300,000 people from the balcony of the presidential palace, and promised to lead the people to victory in the coming presidential election. Four days later, Peron, a widower, married Eva Duarte, or "Evita," as she became affectionately known.

Nuremberg Trials
- Held for the purpose of bringing Nazi war criminals to justice, the Nuremberg trials were a series of 13 trials carried out in Nuremberg, Germany, between 1945 and 1949. The defendants, who included Nazi Party officials and high-ranking military officers along with German industrialists, lawyers and doctors, were indicted on such charges as crimes against peace and crimes against humanity.

Winston Churchill Gives His "Iron Curtain" Speech
- In one of the most famous orations of the Cold War period, former British Prime Minister Winston Churchill condemns the Soviet Union's

policies in Europe and declares, "From Stettin in the Baltic to Trieste in the Adriatic, an iron curtain has descended across the continent." Churchill's speech is considered one of the opening volleys announcing the beginning of the Cold War.

1947

Chuck Yeager Breaks the Sound Barrier
- U.S. Air Force Captain Chuck Yeager becomes the first person to fly faster than the speed of sound.
- Yeager, born in Myra, West Virginia, in 1923, was a combat fighter during World War II and flew 64 missions over Europe. He shot down 13 German planes and was himself shot down over France, but he escaped capture with the assistance of the French Underground. After the war, he was among several volunteers chosen to test-fly the experimental X-1 rocket plane, built by the Bell Aircraft Company to explore the possibility of supersonic flight.

Dead Sea Scrolls Discovered
- The Dead Sea scrolls are one of the greatest discoveries in archaeological history. The ancient texts first came to light in 1947, when a young goat herder stumbled upon some

manuscripts hidden in a cave at Khirbat Qumrān—about a dozen miles (19 kilometers) from the ancient West Bank city of Jericho.

Jewish Refugees Aboard the Exodus Turned Back by British

- Exodus 1947 was a ship that carried Jewish emigrants from France to British Mandatory Palestine on July 11, 1947. Most of the emigrants were Holocaust survivors who had no legal immigration certificates for Palestine. Following wide media coverage, the British Royal Navy seized the ship and deported all its passengers back to Europe.

Marshall Plan

- The Marshall Plan, also known as the European Recovery Program, channeled over $13 billion to finance the economic recovery of Europe between 1948 and 1951. The Marshall Plan successfully sparked economic recovery, meeting its objective of 'restoring the confidence of the European people in the economic future of their own countries and of Europe as a whole.' The plan is named for Secretary of State George C. Marshall, who announced it in a commencement speech at Harvard University on June 5, 1947.

Polaroid Cameras Invented

- Polaroid founder Edwin Land first demonstrated the instant camera on February 21, 1947 at a meeting of the Optical Society of America in New York City.
- The Land camera, as it was originally known, contained a roll of positive paper with a pod of developing chemicals at the top of each frame. Turning a knob forced the exposed negative and paper through rollers, which spread the reagents evenly between the two layers and pushed it out of the camera. A paper cutter trimmed the paper and after a minute the layers could be peeled apart to reveal the black-and-white photo.

1948

Berlin Airlift

- On June 24, 1948, the Soviet Union blocked all road and rail travel to and from West Berlin, which was located within the Soviet zone of occupation in Germany. The Soviet action was in response to the refusal of American and British officials to allow Russia more say in the economic future of Germany. The U.S. government was shocked by the provocative Soviet move, and some in President Harry S. Truman's administration called for a direct military response. Truman, however, did not want to cause World War III. Instead, he ordered a massive airlift of supplies into West Berlin. On June 26, 1948, the first planes took off from bases in England and western Germany and landed in West Berlin. It was a daunting logistical task to provide food, clothing, water, medicine, and other necessities of life for the over 2 million fearful citizens of the city. For nearly a year, American planes landed around the clock. Over 200,000 planes carried in more than one-and-a-half million tons of supplies.

"Big Bang" Theory Formulated

- The seeds of the Big Bang theory were laid by the Alexander Friedmann, who had the courage to examine the full implications of Einstein's general theory of relativity for cosmology—that the universe may not be static. It could be expanding or contracting. Few people took Friedmann seriously and his work was little known. The idea was independently proposed by Georges Lemaître, a Belgian Priest, whose theory that the universe began with the decay of a single atom was also found wanting because it, too, could not explain how hydrogen and helium, the building blocks of the other elements, were formed.

Inventions & Events

"Dewey Defeats Truman" in the Newspaper

- Arguably the most famous headline in the newspaper's 150-year history, DEWEY DEFEATS TRUMAN is every publisher's nightmare on every election night. Like most newspapers, the Tribune, which had dismissed him on its editorial page as a "nincompoop," was lulled into a false sense of security by polls that repeatedly predicted a Dewey victory. Critically important, though, was a printers' strike, which forced the paper to go to press hours before it normally would. As the first-edition deadline approached, managing editor J. Loy "Pat" Maloney had to make the headline call, although many East Coast tallies were not yet in. Maloney banked on the track record of Arthur Sears Henning, the paper's longtime Washington correspondent. Henning said Dewey. Henning was rarely wrong. Besides, Life magazine had just carried a big photo of Dewey with the caption "The next President of the United States.

"Gandhi Assassinated

- Mohandas Karamchand Gandhi (often called Mahatma Gandhi in India) was assassinated on 30 January 1948, shot at point-blank range by Nathuram Godse. Gandhi was outside on the steps of a building where a prayer meeting was going to take place. He was surrounded by a part of his family and some followers when three gunshots killed him. Prior to his death, there had been five unsuccessful attempts to kill Gandhi, the first occurring in 1934.

Policy of Apartheid Begun
- After the National Party gained power in South Africa in 1948, its all-white government immediately began enforcing existing policies of racial segregation under a system of legislation that it called apartheid. Under apartheid, non-white South Africans (a majority of the population) would be forced to live in separate areas from whites and use separate public facilities, and contact between the two groups would be limited. Despite strong and consistent opposition to apartheid within and outside of South Africa, its laws remained in effect for the better part of 50 years. In 1991, the government of President F.W. de Klerk began to repeal most of the legislation that provided the basis for apartheid.

State of Israel Founded
- On May 14, 1948, David Ben-Gurion, the head of the Jewish Agency, proclaimed the establishment of the State of Israel. U.S. President Harry S. Truman recognized the new nation on the same day.

1949

China Becomes Communist
- In October 1949, Mao had declared the People's Republic of China at the Gate of Heavenly Peace in Beijing.

First Non-Stop Flight Around the World
- After 94 hours, 1 minute of flying time, a Boeing B-50 named Lucky Lady II lands at Carswell Air Force Base, Texas, completing the first ever nonstop, around-the-world trip by an airplane.
- The flight covered 23,452 miles, averaging a ground speed of 249 miles per hour. The modified bomber required air-to-air refueling four times as it flew ever eastward.

George Orwell Publishes Nineteen Eight-Four
- June 6, George Orwell's novel of a dystopian future, Nineteen Eighty-four, is published. The novel's all-seeing leader, known as "Big Brother," becomes a universal symbol for intrusive government and oppressive bureaucracy.

NATO Established
- April 4, The North Atlantic Treaty Organization (NATO) is established by 12 Western nations: the United States, Great Britain, France, Belgium, the Netherlands, Denmark, Italy, Luxembourg, Norway, Iceland, Canada, and Portugal. The military alliance, which provided for a collective self-defense against Soviet aggression, greatly increased American influence in Europe.

Soviet Union Has Atomic Bomb
- Aug. 29, at a remote test site at Semipalatinsk in Kazakhstan, the USSR successfully detonates its first atomic bomb, code name "First Lightning." In order to measure the effects of the blast, the Soviet scientists constructed buildings, bridges, and other civilian structures in the vicinity of the bomb. They also placed animals in cages nearby so that they could test the effects of nuclear radiation on human-like mammals. The atomic explosion, which at 20 kilotons was roughly equal to "Trinity," the first U.S. atomic explosion, destroyed those structures and incinerated the animals.

The 40's were stuffed with war and hardship. After '45 we all were hoping to get our lives back on track, but war stepped in the way again.

Inventions & Events

The 50's started off with the Korean War that cost 30,000 American lives.

Building the American Dream

Truman - 45 - 52

Eisenhower - 52 - 60

1950 - 1959 - Inventions & Events

1950

First Modern Credit Card Introduced
- First Modern Credit Card Introduced (1950): In 1949, Frank X. McNamara thought of a way for customers to have just one credit card that they could use at multiple stores. McNamara discussed the idea with two colleagues and the three pooled some money and started a

Inventions & Events

new company in 1950 which they called the Diners Club.
- The first Diners Club credit cards were given out in 1950 to 200 people (most were friends and acquaintances of McNamara) and accepted by 14 restaurants in New York. The concept of the card grew and by the end of 1950, 20,000 people were using the Diners Club credit card. The Diners Club credit card is considered the first modern credit card.

First Organ Transplant
- Ruth Tucker, 49, suffered from polycystic kidneys and was in need of a new kidney. One of her kidneys was non-functioning and the other only functioned at 10 percent. Tucker's mother and sister had also died from the same disease. The doctors, hospital leadership and patient bravely decided to attempt something that hadn't been done before—an organ transplant. History was made at Little Company of Mary Hospital on June 17, 1950, when doctors performed the first successful organ transplant in the world.

First "Peanuts" Cartoon Strip
- The very first Peanuts comic strip, written by Charles M. Schulz, appeared in seven newspapers on October 2, 1950.

Korean War Begins
- On June 25, 1950, North Korean forces surprised the South Korean army (and the small U.S. force stationed in the country), and quickly headed toward the capital city of Seoul. The United States responded by pushing a resolution through the U.N.'s Security Council calling for military assistance to South Korea. (Russia was not present to veto the action as it was boycotting the Security Council at the time.) With this resolution in hand, President Harry S. Truman rapidly dispatched U.S. land, air, and sea forces to Korea to engage in what he termed a "police action." The American intervention turned the tide, and U.S. and South Korean forces marched into North Korea. This action, however, prompted the massive intervention of communist Chinese forces in late 1950. The war in Korea subsequently bogged down into a bloody stalemate. In 1953, the United States and North Korea signed a cease-fire that ended the conflict.

Senator Joseph McCarthy Begins Communist Witch Hunt
- Nearing the end of his term after being elected in 1943, Senator Joseph McCarthy's

first term was criticized as unimpressive. McCarthy searched for ways to keep his political success alive, a Roman-Catholic friend by the name of Edmund Walsh, suggested a "crusade" against so-called underground communist. McCarthy agreed and took advantage of the nations wave of terror against communism, and on February 9th, 1950, McCarthy came forth with a list of people in the State Department who were known members of the American Communist Party. The American public then went crazy over the thought of communists living within the United States, and urged for the investigation of the underground advocates. Some of the people on the list were in fact not communist. Regardless, for two years McCarthy continued to interrogate and question innocent citizens and multiple government departments, the panic rising from the so called "witch-hunts" and fear of communism became known as McCarthyism.

U.S. President Truman Orders Construction of Hydrogen Bomb

- On January 31st, 1950, Truman announced that he had directed the Atomic Agency Commission 'to continue with its work on all forms of atomic energy weapons, including the so-called hydrogen or super-bomb'.

1951

Color TV Introduced
- On June 25, 1951, CBS broadcast the very first commercial color TV program. Unfortunately, nearly no one could watch it on their black-and-white televisions.

South Africans Forced to Carry ID Cards Identifying Race
- Population Registration Act, Act No 30 of 1950 Led to the creation of a national register in which every person's race was recorded. A Race Classification Board took the final decision on what a person's race was in disputed cases.

Truman Signs Peace Treaty With Japan, Officially Ending WWII
- The Treaty of Peace with Japan (commonly known as the Treaty of San Francisco, Peace Treaty of San Francisco, or San Francisco Peace Treaty), between Japan and part of the Allied Powers, was officially signed by 48 nations on September 8, 1951, at the War Memorial Opera House in San Francisco, United States. It came into force on April 28, 1952.

Winston Churchill Again Prime Minister of Great Britain

- Winston Churchill Again Prime Minister of Great Britain (1951): After being chosen to be Prime Minister of Great Britain in 1940 to lead the country during World War II, Winston Churchill refused to surrender to the Germans, built up British morale, and became a central force of the Allies. However, before the war with Japan had ended, Churchill and his Conservative Party were soundly defeated by the Labour Party in a general election held in July 1945.
- Considering Churchill's near-hero status at the time, it was a shock that Churchill lost the election. The public, although grateful to Churchill for his role in winning the war, was ready for change. After half a decade at war, the populace was ready to think of the future. The Labour Party, who focused on domestic rather than foreign issues, included in its platform programs for such things as better health care and education.
- Six years later, in another general election, the Conservative Party won the majority of seats. With this win, Winston Churchill became Prime Minister of Great Britain for his second term in 1951.
- On April 5, 1955, at age 80, Churchill resigned as Prime Minister.

1952

Car Seat Belts Introduced
- A seat belt, also known as a safety belt, is a vehicle safety device designed to secure the occupant of a vehicle against harmful movement that may result during a collision or a sudden stop.

The Great Smog of 1952
- When a thick fog engulfed London from December 5 to December 9, 1952, it mixed with black smoke emitted from homes and factories to create a deadly smog. This smog killed approximately 12,000 people and shocked the world into starting the environmental movement.

Jacques Cousteau Discovers Ancient Greek Ship
- In July, 1952, Calypso left Toulon for Marseilles. She shuttled back and forth to the little islet of Grand Congloué where the team was studying a shipwreck from the third century BC, lying 40 meters underwater. That was when a young Albert Falco joined the crew. Thousands of amphorae and pottery shards were brought to the surface and taken back to the Borely Muse-

um and the Roman Docks Museum of Marseilles.

Polio Vaccine Created
•   Poliomyelitis has been around since ancient times. There is still no cure for the disease. But at the peak of its devastation in the United States, Jonas Salk introduced a way to prevent it. This infectious viral disease attacks the nerve cells and sometimes the central nervous system, often causing muscle wasting and paralysis and even death. Since 1900 there had been cycles of epidemics, each seeming to get stronger and more disastrous. The disease, whose early symptoms are like the flu, struck mostly children, although adults, including Franklin Roosevelt, caught it too.

Princess Elizabeth Becomes Queen at Age 25
•   After suffering from lung cancer for several years, King George VI died in his sleep on February 6, 1952 at age 56. Upon his death, his oldest daughter, Princess Elizabeth, became queen. Elizabeth was 25 years old.

1953

DNA Discovered
- The sentence "This structure has novel features which are of considerable biological interest" may be one of science's most famous understatements. It appeared in April 1953 in the scientific paper where James Watson and Francis Crick presented the structure of the DNA-helix, the molecule that carries genetic information from one generation to the other.
- Nine years later, in 1962, they shared the Nobel Prize in Physiology or Medicine with Maurice Wilkins, for solving one of the most important of all biological riddles. Half a century later, important new implications of this contribution to science are still coming to light.First Playboy Magazine

Hillary and Norgay Climb Mt. Everest
- After years of dreaming about it and seven weeks of climbing, New Zealander Edmund Hillary and Nepalese Tenzing Norgay reached the top of Mount Everest, the highest mountain in the world, at 11:30 a.m. on May 29, 1953. They were the first people to ever reach the summit of Mount Everest.

Joseph Stalin Dies

- On this day, March 5, Joseph Stalin, leader of the Soviet Union since 1924, dies in Moscow.
- Like his right-wing counterpart, Hitler, who was born in Austria, Joseph Stalin was not a native of the country he ruled with an iron fist. Isoeb Dzhugashvili was born in 1889 in Georgia, then part of the old Russian empire. The son of a drunk who beat him mercilessly and a pious washerwoman mother, Stalin learned Russian, which he spoke with a heavy accent all his life, in an Orthodox Church-run school. While studying to be a priest at Tiflis Theological Seminary, he began secretly reading Karl Marx and other left-wing revolutionary thinkers. The "official" communist story is that he was expelled from the seminary for this intellectual rebellion; in reality, it may have been because of poor health.

Julius and Ethel Rosenberg Executed for Espionage

- Julius and Ethel Rosenberg, a married couple convicted of conspiracy to commit espionage in 1951, are put to death in the electric chair. The execution marked the dramatic finale of the most controversial espionage case of the Cold War.

Inventions & Events

- Julius was arrested in July 1950, and Ethel in August of that same year, on the charge of conspiracy to commit espionage. Specifically, they were accused of heading a spy ring that passed top-secret information concerning the atomic bomb to the Soviet Union. The Rosenbergs vigorously protested their innocence, but after a brief trial in March 1951 they were convicted. On April 5, 1951, a judge sentenced them to death. The pair was taken to Sing Sing Prison in Ossining, New York, to await execution. During the next two years, the couple became the subject of both national and international debate. Many people believed that the Rosenbergs were the victims of a surge of hysterical anti-communist feeling in the United States, and protested that the death sentence handed down was cruel and unusual punishment. Most Americans, however, believed that the Rosenbergs had been dealt with justly. President Dwight D. Eisenhower spoke for many Americans when he issued a statement declining to invoke executive clemency for the pair. He stated, "I can only say that, by immeasurably increasing the chances of atomic war, the Rosenbergs may have condemned to death tens of millions of innocent people all over the world. The execution of two human beings is a grave matter. But even graver is the thought of the millions of dead whose deaths may be directly attributable to what these spies have done."

1954

Britain Sponsors an Expedition to Search for the Abominable Snowman

- Sir Edmund continued his mountain climbing expeditions long after his successful ascent of Everest in 1953. During some of these, he found a number of strange things which intrigued him greatly. For example, on one expedition, he came across some curious hair high up on the snowy mountainside. On others, he found huge footprints. His climbing adventures had brought him into contact with the Sherpa people of Nepal. In fact, it was a Sherpa, Tenzing Norgay, who first climbed Everest with him. The Sherpa people had many legends about strange creatures which seemed to be half ape and half man. Their term for these creatures was translated as "Abominable Snowman", sometimes also called a "Yeti", and Tenzing Norgay even claimed to have seen one himself personally.

Inventions & Events

First Atomic Submarine Launched
- On January 21, 1954, Nautilus was christened by First Lady Mamie Eisenhower and launched into the Thames River.

Report Says Cigarettes Cause Cancer
- On January 4, 1954, in response to continuing scientific reports on the health effects of smoking, "the TIRC ... ran a full-page promotion in more than 400 newspapers aimed at an estimated 43 million Americans," according to papers filed in the 1995 Florida Medicaid lawsuit.

Roger Bannister Breaks the Four-Minute Mile
- On this day, May 6, at the Iffley Road Track in Oxford, England, medical student Roger Bannister becomes the first person in recorded history to run the mile in under four minutes.

Segregation Ruled Illegal in U.S.
- On May 17, 1954, the law was changed. In the landmark Supreme Court decision of Brown v. Board of Education, the Supreme Court overturned the Plessy v. Ferguson decision by ruling that segregation was "inherently unequal." Although the Brown v. Board of Education was specifically for the field of education, the decision had a much broader scope.

- Although the Brown v. Board of Education decision overturned all the segregation laws in the country, the enactment of integration was not immediate. In actuality, it took many years, much turmoil, and even bloodshed to integrate the country.

1955

Disneyland Opens

- Disneyland, Walt Disney's metropolis of nostalgia, fantasy, and futurism, opens on July 17, 1955. The $17 million theme park was built on 160 acres of former orange groves in Anaheim, California, and soon brought in staggering profits. Today, Disneyland hosts more than 14 million visitors a year, who spend close to $3 billion.

Emmett Till Murdered

- On March 30, the Federal Bureau of Investigation publicly released its 2006 report on the Emmett Till case. In 1955, Till, a black teenager from Chicago, went to Mississippi to visit relatives. During a trip to a store, he whistled at a white woman named Carolyn Bryant, the wife of the store's owner. Shortly thereafter, Mrs. Bryant's husband Roy and her brother-in-law J.W. Milam kidnapped Till. Emmett's mangled body was found a few days later. A local jury acquitted Milam and Bryant of murder, but the pair later acknowledged that they had slain the fourteen-year-old Till. The two admitted murderers are both dead, but evidence recently uncovered by filmmaker Keith Beauchamp indicated to federal authorities that there might have been other perpetrators who remained alive.

James Dean Dies in Car Accident
- On September 30, 1955, actor James Dean was driving his new Porsche 550 Spyder to an auto rally in Salinas, California when he was involved in a head-on collision with a 1950 Ford Tutor. James Dean, only 24 years old, died in the crash. Although already famous for his role in East of Eden, his death and the release of Rebel Without a Cause caused James Dean to soar to cult status. James Dean, forever frozen as the talented, misunderstood, rebellious youth, remains the symbol of teenage angst.

McDonald's Corporation Founded
- Kroc pitched his vision of creating McDonald's restaurants all over the U.S. to the brothers. In 1955 he founded the McDonald's Corporation, and 5 years later bought the exclusive rights to the McDonald's name. By 1958,

McDonald's had sold its 100 millionth hamburger.

Rosa Parks Refuses to Give Up Her Seat on a Bus

- On December 1, 1955, Rosa Parks, a 42-year-old African-American seamstress, refused to give up her seat to a white man while riding on a city bus in Montgomery, Alabama. For doing this, Rosa Parks was arrested and fined for breaking the laws of segregation. Rosa Parks' refusal to leave her seat sparked the Montgomery Bus Boycott and is considered the beginning of the modern Civil Rights Movement.

Warsaw Pact Signed

- On May 14, the Soviet Union and seven of its European satellites sign a treaty establishing the Warsaw Pact, a mutual defense organization that put the Soviets in command of the armed forces of the member states.

Ron Berger enlisted in the USAF

- July 5 - I thought it was important.

1956

Elvis Gyrates on Ed Sullivan's Show
- Elvis Presley had already appeared on other national television shows (such as on Stage Show, The Milton Berle Show, and on the popular The Steve Allen Show) when Ed Sullivan booked Elvis for three shows. Elvis' pelvic gyrations during his appearances on these other shows had caused much discussion and concern about the suitability of airing such provocative and sensual movements on television.

Grace Kelly Marries Prince Rainier III of Monaco
- American actress Grace Patricia Kelly married Prince Rainier III of Monaco in 1956 in two separate ceremonies: a civil ceremony on 18 April and in a Catholic Mass on 19 April. The wedding was called "The Wedding of the Century" and is still considered one of the most beautiful weddings ever.

Hungarian Revolution
- A spontaneous nationwide revolt against the government of the People's Republic of Hungary and its Soviet-imposed policies, lasting from 23 October until 10 November 1956. It was the first major threat to Soviet control since the USSR's forces drove out the Nazis at the end of World War II and occupied Eastern Europe. De-

spite the failure of the uprising, it was highly influential, and came to play a role in the downfall of the Soviet Union decades later.

Khrushchev Denounces Stalin

- For thirty years, Joseph Stalin had ruled the Soviet Union unchallenged. Less than three years after his death, new Soviet premier Nikita Khrushchev shocked the Twentieth Communist Party Congress with a long, angry speech that denounced Stalin.
- Khrushchev framed his attack as a critique of the dead leader for promoting the "cult of personality," which, he said, is alien to Marxism-Leninism. He began dismantling Stalin's claims to greatness by pointing out that Soviet founder Vladimir Lenin had written in his will that Stalin should be removed from his position as secretary general of the Communist Party. Khrushchev revealed Lenin's trenchant criticisms of Stalin, which Stalin had managed to suppress.

Suez Crisis

- On July 26, 1956, Egyptian President Gamal Abdel Nasser announced the nationalization of the Suez Canal Company, the joint British-French enterprise which had owned and operated the Suez Canal since its construction in 1869. Nasser's announcement came about following months of mounting political tensions between Egypt, Britain, and France. Although Nasser offered full economic compensation for the Company, the British and French Governments, long suspicious of Nasser's opposition to the continuation of their political influence in the region, were outraged by the nationalization. The Egyptian leader, in turn, resented what he saw as European efforts to perpetuate their colonial domination.

T.V. Remote Control Invented

- It was in June of 1956, that the practical television remote controller first entered the American home. However, as far back as 1893, a remote control for television was described by Nikola Tesla in U.S. Patent 613809. The Germans used remote control motorboats during WWI. In the late 1940's the first non-military uses for remote controls appeared for example, automatic garage door openers.

Velcro Introduced

- Hook-and-loop fasteners consist of two components: typically, two lineal fabric strips (or, alternatively, round "dots" or squares) which are attached (e.g., sewn, adhered, etc.) to the opposing surfaces to be fastened. The first component features tiny hooks; the second features even smaller and "hairier" loops. When the two components are pressed together, the hooks catch in the loops and the two pieces fasten or bind temporarily during the time that they are pressed together.[4] When separated, by pulling or peeling the two surfaces apart, the velcro strips make a distinctive "ripping" sound.

1957

Dr. Seuss Publishes The Cat in the Hat

- The Cat in the Hat is a children's book written and illustrated by Theodor Geisel under the pen name Dr. Seuss and first published in 1957. The story centers on a tall anthropomorphic cat, who wears a red and white-striped hat and a red bow tie. The Cat shows up at the house of Sally and her brother one rainy day when their mother is away. Ignoring repeated objections from the children's fish, the Cat shows the children a few of his tricks in an attempt to entertain them. In the process he and his companions, Thing One and Thing Two, wreck the house. The children and the fish become more and more alarmed until the Cat produces a machine that he uses to clean everything up. He then disappears just before the children's mother walks in.

European Economic Community Established
•   The EEC Treaty, signed in Rome in 1957, brings together France, Germany, Italy and the Benelux countries in a community whose aim is to achieve integration via trade with a view to economic expansion. After the Treaty of Maastricht the EEC became the European Community, reflecting the determination of the Member States to expand the Community's powers to non-economic domains.

Soviet Satellite Sputnik Launches Space Age
•   History changed on October 4, 1957, when the Soviet Union successfully launched Sputnik I. The world's first artificial satellite was about the size of a beach ball (58 cm.or 22.8 inches in diameter), weighed only 83.6 kg. or 183.9 pounds, and took about 98 minutes to orbit the Earth on its elliptical path. That launch ushered in new political, military, technological, and scientific developments. While the Sputnik launch was a single event, it marked the start of the space age and the U.S.-U.S.S.R space race.

Laika Becomes the First Living Animal to Enter Orbit
•   The Soviet Union and the United States were in a very heated competition after World

War II. Part of this competition was over control of space. As part of this "space race," the Soviets succeeded in putting up the first satellite into space in October 1957. Working hastily, the Soviets launched their second satellite (Sputnik 2) on November 3, 1957 with a living animal (Laika the dog) on board. Laika lived through the launch, but died in space since no return plan had been created for her.

1958

Boris Pasternak Refuses Nobel Prize
- This year's Nobel Prize for Literature has been awarded by the Swedish Academy to the Soviet-Russian writer Boris Pasternak for his notable achievement in both contemporary poetry and the field of the great Russian narrative tradition.
- As is well known, Pasternak has sent word that he does not wish to accept the distinction. This refusal, of course, in no way alters the validity of the award. There remains only for the Academy, however, to announce with regret that the presentation of the Prize cannot take place.

Chinese Leader Mao Zedong Launches the "Great Leap Forward"

- The Great Leap Forward was a push by Mao Zedong to change China from a predominantly agrarian (farming) society to a modern, industrial society in just five years.

Hope Diamond is Donated to the Smithsonian

- On November 10, 1958, they donated the Hope diamond to the Smithsonian Institution, and almost immediately the great blue stone became its premier attraction.

Hula Hoops Become Popular

- A hula hoop is a company toy hoop that is twirled around the waist, limbs or neck. The modern hula hoop was invented in 1958 by Arthur K. Melin and Richard Knerr, but children and adults around the world have played with hoops, twirling, rolling and throwing them throughout history.

LEGO Toy Bricks First Introduced

- In 1953, the Automatic Binding Bricks were renamed LEGO Bricks and in 1958, these bricks underwent a slight change in their design, which transformed them into the LEGO Bricks we know today.

NASA Founded

- July 29, the United States Congress passes legislation formally inaugurating the National Aeronautics and Space Administration (NASA). The establishment of NASA was a sign that the United States was committed to winning the "space race" against the Soviets.

Peace Symbol Created

- In 1958, British artist Gerald Holtom drew a circle with three lines inside, intending the design to be a symbol for the Direct Action Committee Against Nuclear War (DAC). The design incorporates a circle with the lines within it representing the simplified positions of two semaphore letters (the system of using flags to send information great distances, such as from ship to ship). The letters "N" and "D" were used to represent "nuclear disarmament." (The "N" is formed by a person holding a flag in each hand and then pointing them toward the ground at a 45 degree angle. The "D" is formed by holding one flag straight down and one straight up.)

1959

Castro Becomes Dictator of Cuba

- On January 1, 1959, Batista admitted defeat and left the country. Although not at first appointed president, Castro succeeded in taking power of the new Cuban government by July 1959.

International Treaty Makes Antarctica Scientific Preserve
- On Dec. 1, 1959, representatives of 12 countries, including the United States and the Soviet Union, signed a treaty in Washington, which designated Antarctica as a scientific preserve, free from military activity.

Ron Berger Discharged July 4
- Couldn't help throwing that in

Kitchen Debate Between Nixon and Khrushchev
- July 24, during the grand opening ceremony of the American National Exhibition in Moscow, Vice President Richard Nixon and Soviet leader Nikita Khrushchev engage in a heated debate about capitalism and communism in the middle of a model kitchen set up for the fair. The so-called "kitchen debate" became one of the most famous episodes of the Cold War.

The Sound of Music Opens on Broadway

- The Story of the Trapp Family Singers, were ignored by the creators of the Broadway musical her memoir inspired. And while the liberties taken by the show's writers, Howard Lindsay and Russel Crouse, and by its composer and lyricist, Richard Rodgers and Oscar Hammerstein II, caused some consternation to the real Maria von Trapp and to her stepchildren, according to many later reports, those liberties made The Sound of Music a smash success from the very night of its Broadway opening on this day in 1959.

U.S. Quiz Shows Found to be Fixed

- Herb Stempel was a contestant on Twenty One who was coached by the show's producer Dan Enright. While Stempel was in the midst of his winning streak, both of the $64,000 quiz shows were in the top-ten rated programs but Twenty One did not have the same popularity. Enright and his partner Albert Freedman were searching for a new champion to replace Stempel to boost ratings. They soon found what they were looking for in Charles Lincoln Van Doren. Charles Van Doren was an English teacher at Columbia University when a friend suggested he try out for a quiz show. Skeptical at first, Van Doren decided to try out for the quiz show Tic-Tac-Dough because of the possible money a contestant could win. Enright, who produced both Tic-Tac-Dough and Twenty One, saw Van Doren's tryout and was familiar with his prestigious family background that included multiple Pulitzer Prize-winning authors and highly respected professors at Columbia University. As a result, Enright felt that Van Doren would be the perfect contestant to be the new face of Twenty One.[6]

- As part of their plan, the producers of Twenty One arranged the first Van Doren-Stempel face-off to end in three ties. This strategy paid off as millions of viewers tuned in the next evening to watch. Although the manipulation of the contestants on Twenty One helped the producers maintain viewer interest and ratings, the producers had not anticipated the extent of Stempel's resentment at being required to lose the contest against Van Doren.[7] After achieving winnings of $69,500, Stempel's scripted loss to the more popular Van Doren occurred on 5 December 1956. One of the questions Stempel answered incorrectly involved the winner of the 1955 Academy Award for Best Motion Picture. (The correct answer was Marty, one of Stempel's favorite movies; as instructed by Enright, Stempel gave the incorrect answer On the Waterfront, winner of Best Picture the previous year.) After his preordained loss, Stempel spoke out against the operation, claiming that he deliberately lost the match against Van Doren on orders from Enright.

The 50's were the beginning of big things in America. We got over the Korean War and started turning our attention to our lifestyle. Automobiles, houses, gadgets, music, etc, were on the agenda. It was a great time growing up.

Inventions & Events

JFK - 60 - 63   LBJ - 63 - 68   Nixon - 68 - 74

1960 - 1969 - Inventions

1960

The 60s have been described by historians as the ten years having the most significant changes in history. By the end of the 60s humanity had entered the spaceage by putting a man on the moon. The 60s were influenced by the youth of the post-war baby boom - a generation with a fondness for change and far-out gadgets.

The halogen lamp invented.
- The halogen lamp is also known as a quartz halogen and tungsten halogen lamp. It is an advanced form of incandescent lamp. The

filament is composed of ductile tungsten and located in a gas filled bulb just like a standard tungsten bulb, however the gas in a halogen bulb is at a higher pressure (7-8 ATM). The glass bulb is made of fused quartz, high-silica glass or aluminosilicate. This bulb is stronger than standard glass in order to contain the high pressure. This lamp has been an industry standard for work lights and film/television lighting due to compact size and high lumen output. The halogen lamp is being replaced slowly by the white LED array lamp, miniature HID and fluorescent lamps. Increased efficiency halogens with 30+ lumens per watt may change sale decline in the future.

1961

Valium invented.
- The discovery was an impressive achievement for a project he was not even supposed to be working on.
- The saga began in 1953 when Wallace Pharmaceuticals brought out an anti-anxiety drug called Miltown that was then thought -- wrongly, it was learned later -- to be free of the many adverse side effects that afflicted barbiturates, the most widely used drugs for anxiety at the time.

- Sternbach's bosses at Roche in New Jersey ordered him to produce a "me too" version of Miltown by modifying the drug enough to bypass Wallace's patents. Sternbach, however, thought modifying another man's drug was boring.
- Instead, he followed a hunch about some compounds he had studied as potential dyes years earlier in Poland. Their structures, he reasoned, could interact favorably with the human nervous system.
- But two years of research proved fruitless, and his bosses told him to drop the project and switch to the development of antibiotics. Sternbach began working on the germ-killers, but he kept tinkering with the dyes. "I always did what I wanted to do," he later said.
- Within two years, he and his colleagues -- especially chemist Earl Reeder -- had discovered the first benzodiazepine. As they did with other potential anti-anxiety drugs, they tested it on mice that were placed at the bottom of a steeply inclined screen. Normal mice climb the screen easily. Drugged mice relax and slide back down, where they mingle in a group torpor.
- With the new drug, the mice also relaxed and slid back down. But even at the bottom, they were awake and alert, a remarkable thing.
- Because he was not supposed to be working on anti-anxiety drugs, Sternbach sat on the discov-

ery for six months. Finally, using the excuse of a periodic laboratory cleanup, he presented it to Lowell Randall, Roche's chief of pharmacology, as something they had stumbled across that should be tested.
- A few days later, Randall called back to say the compound was "interesting" and asked for more. The drug was Librium, which went on the market in 1960.
- Three years later, the company brought out Valium, also discovered by Sternbach, as the successor to Librium. Valium was the biggest-selling drug in the country from 1969 to 1980, but it lost some of its luster when it was found to be addictive.

The nondairy creamer invented.
- Nondairy creamers (also called "coffee whiteners") are liquid or granular substances intended to substitute for milk or cream as an additive to coffee or other beverages. They do not contain lactose and therefore are commonly described as not being dairy products (although many contain casein, a milk-derived protein).

1962

The audio cassette invented.
- In 1962 Philips was the first company to invent the compact audio cassette medium size for audio storage. However, this success begun in Germany by AEG in 1935 when it released reel-to-reel tape recorder, this development was based on an earlier invention of the magnetic tape in 1928 by Fritz Pfleumer.

The fiber-tip pen invented by Yukio Horie.
- A marker pen, marking pen, felt-tip pen, flow, marker or texta (in Australia), is a pen which has its own ink-source, and usually a tip made of a porous, pressed fibers such as felt.[1] A typical permanent marker consists of a container (glass, aluminum or plastic) and a core of an absorbent material. This filling serves as a carrier for the ink. The upper part of the marker contains the nib that was made in earlier time of a hard felt material, and a cap to prevent the marker from drying out.

Spacewar, the first computer video game invented.
- It was in 1962 when a young computer programmer from MIT, Steve Russell fueled with inspiration from the writings of E. E. "Doc" Smith*, led the team** that created the first popular computer game. Starwar was almost the

first computer game ever written, however, they were at least two far-lesser known predecessors: OXO (1952) and Tennis for Two (1958).

Dow Corp invents silicone breast implants.
- The first silicone breast implant was invented in 1962. This invention was done by a plastic surgeon in Texas named Thomas Cronin. In 1965, the first saline implant was created by a French plastic surgeon named H.R. Arion.

1963

The video disk invented.
- Steve "Slug" Russell (born 1937) is an American computer scientist most famous for creating Spacewar!, one of the earliest video games.

1964

Acrylic paint invented.
- Acrylic paint is fast-drying paint containing pigment suspension in acrylic polymer emulsion. Acrylic paints can be diluted with water, but become water-resistant when dry. Depending on how much the paint is diluted (with water) or modified with acrylic gels, media, or pastes, the finished acrylic painting can resemble a water-

color or an oil painting, or have its own unique characteristics not attainable with other media.

Permanent-press fabric invented.
- Half a century ago, working quietly in a New Orleans laboratory, Ruth Benerito helped smooth the fabric of modern life. In so doing, she helped liberate people from hours of household drudgery.
- A chemist long affiliated with the United States Department of Agriculture, Dr. Benerito helped perfect modern wrinkle-free cotton, colloquially known as permanent press, in work that she and her colleagues began in the late 1950s.
- Widely available since the mid-1960s, wrinkle-free cotton is considered one of the most significant technological developments of the 20th century. For her role, Dr. Benerito was inducted into the National Inventors Hall of Fame in 2008.

BASIC (an early computer language) is invented by John George Kemeny and Tom Kurtz.
- John George Kemeny (Hungarian: Kemény János György; May 31, 1926[1] – December 26, 1992) was a Jewish-Hungarian American mathematician, computer scientist, and educator best known for co-developing[2] the BASIC programming language in 1964 with Thomas E.

Kurtz. Kemeny served as the 13th President of Dartmouth College from 1970 to 1981 and pioneered the use of computers in college education. Kemeny chaired the presidential commission that investigated the Three Mile Island accident in 1979.[

1965

Astroturf invented.
•   James Faria and Robert Wright of Monsanto Industries co-invented Astroturf. A patent for astroturf was filed for on December 25, 1965 and issued by the USPTO on July 25, 1967.

Soft contact lenses invented.
•   The world's first soft lens conference was held in Prague. Many of the early problems with the material were sorted out.

NutraSweet invented.
•   The NutraSweet Company makes and sells NutraSweet, their trademarked brand name for the artificial sweetener aspartame, and Neotame. Despite losing market share in recent years to sucralose, the NutraSweet Company states that its product is used in more than 5,000 products and consumed by some 250 million people worldwide.

- Aspartame was invented by chemists at G. D. Searle & Company in 1965. Searle was bought by Monsanto in 1985. In March 2000, Monsanto, which was then a subsidiary of the Pharmacia corporation, sold NutraSweet to the private equity firm J.W. Childs.

The compact disk invented by James Russell.
- A compact disk (cd) is a popular form of digital storage media used for computer files, pictures, and music. The plastic platter is read and written to by a laser in a CD drive. It comes in several varieties including CD-ROM, CD-R, and CD-RW.
- James Russell invented the compact disk in 1965. James Russell was granted a total of 22 patents for various elements of his compact disk system. However, the compact disk did not become popular until it was mass manufactured by Philips in 1980.

Kevlar invented by Stephanie Louise Kwolek.
- In 1965 Stephanie L. Kwolek (b. 1923) succeeded in creating the first of a family of synthetic fibers of exceptional strength and stiffness. The best known member is Kevlar, a material used in fragmentation-resistant vests as well as in boats, airplanes, ropes, cables, tires,

tennis racquets, skis, and so forth—in total about 200 applications.

1966

Electronic Fuel injection for cars invented.
- The fuel injector was invented to increase the performance of the engine. The electronic fuel injector, which has replaced the carburetor, provides a better distribution of fuel into the combustion chamber.

1967

The first handheld calculator invented.
- During the early 1960s, Pat Haggerty discussed the possibility of a handheld calculator with Jack Kilby on a business trip. There were other priorities, but in 1964, Dean Toombs, head of semiconductor R&D, formed a team consisting of Kilby, Jim Van Tassel, and Jerry Merryman to develop a calculator small enough to fit in the palm of a hand, yet powerful enough to perform basic math functions.
- By December 1966, the team had a working model, and, within a year, Kilby, Van Tassel, and Merryman filed a patent application, which would be issued eight years later. The functional heart of the first miniature calculator was circuit-

ry able to perform addition, subtraction, multiplication, and division. It had a small keyboard with 18 keys and a visual output that displayed up to 12 decimal digits.

1968

The computer mouse invented by Douglas Engelbart.
- Douglas Engelbart changed the way computers worked, from specialized machinery that only a trained scientist could use, to a user-friendly tool that almost anyone can use. He invented or contributed to several interactive, user-friendly devices: the computer mouse, windows, computer video teleconferencing, hypermedia, groupware, email, the Internet and more.

The first computer with integrated circuits made.
- Texas Instruments had not been able to convince skeptics that integrated circuits were reliable. They thought that if you multiplied the yield of each component in an integrated circuits together, the overall yield would be so low you could never expect to build a good unit. Also, some feared the amount of heat dissipated within a densely packed group of circuits would

keep them from functioning properly. Alberts and Phipps decided TI needed to build a model to demonstrate the viability and reliability of the technology. Alberts backed the project by funding $600,000 enough to let TI build a small digital computer using integrated circuits. It was a bootleg project that Alberts decided to keep secret. The Air Force could not interfere with a project it didnt know existed.

Robert Dennard invented RAM (random access memory).
•   Robert Dennard invented one of the most significant advances in computer technology of modern time—dynamic random access memory, (or DRAM, better known simply as RAM).

1969

The arpanet (first internet) invented.
•   On a cold war kind of day, in swinging 1969, work began on the ARPAnet, grandfather to the Internet. Designed as a computer version of the nuclear bomb shelter, ARPAnet protected the flow of information between military installations by creating a network of geographically separated computers that could exchange information via a newly developed protocol (rule

for how computers interact) called NCP (Network Control Protocol).

The artificial heart invented.
- Robert Jarvik, MD is widely known as the inventor of the first successful permanent artificial heart, the Jarvik 7. In 1982, the first implantation of the Jarvik 7 in patient Barney Clark caught the attention of media around the world. The extraordinary openness of this medical experiment, facilitated by the University of Utah, fueled heated public debate on all aspects of medical research. But as doctors learned how to achieve excellent clinical outcomes in subsequent patients with the Jarvik 7, the press and public largely lost interest in the subject.

The ATM invented.
- Some believe that Luther George Simjian was the inventor because his idea came first. Some believe it was Don Wetzel, after all, he's got patents on display in the Museum of American History to prove it. Still others, including the Queen of England, say the inventor is John Shepherd-Barron. John D. White has contacted ATMmachine.com, sent us copies of patents, and gave convincing evidence that he is the inventor.

- James Goodfellow of Scotland also contacted ATMmachine.com and gave us his account,, including copies of patents. Jairus Larson contacted ATMmachine.com and, although he did not invent the ATM, he did develop the first "on-line" ATM.
- Since the patent on an ATM was never applied for until years after Mr. Simjian, confusion on the inventor still exists. One reason for the confusion is that John Shepherd-Barron lived in the United Kingdom and James Goodfellow in Scotland. While all the others lived in the USA.

The bar-code scanner is invented.
- In 1969, the NAFC asked Logicon, Inc. to develop a proposal for an industry-wide bar code system. The result was Parts 1 and 2 of the Universal Grocery Products Identification Code (UGPIC) in the summer of 1970. Based on the recommendations of the Logicon report, the U.S. Supermarket Ad Hoc Committee on a Uniform Grocery Product Code was formed. Three years later, the Committee recommended the adoption of the UPC symbol set still used in the USA today. It was submitted by IBM and developed by George Laurer, whose work was an outgrowth of the idea of Woodland and Silver. Woodland was an employee at the time of IBM.

1960 - 1969 - Events

1960

Alfred Hitchcock's Psycho Released
- Psycho is a 1960 American suspense horror film directed by Alfred Hitchcock starring Anthony Perkins, Vera Miles, John Gavin, and Janet Leigh. The screenplay is by Joseph Stefano, based on the 1959 novel of the same name by Robert Bloch loosely inspired by the crimes of Wisconsin murderer and grave robber Ed Gein.

Brazil's Capital Moves to Brand New City
- Brasília (Portuguese pronunciation: [bɾaˈziljɐ]) is the federal capital of Brazil and the capital of the Federal District. The city is located along the Brazilian Highlands in the country's Central-West region. It was founded on April 21, 1960, to serve as the new national capital. Brasília had an estimated population of 2,789,761 in 2013, making it the 4th most populous city in Brazil.

First Televised Presidential Debates
- On Sept. 26, 1960, 70 million American viewers watched the first of four televised

presidential debates between candidates Richard Nixon and John F. Kennedy. They were the first debates ever to be held between the presidential nominees of the two major parties during the election season.

Lunch Counter Sit-In at Woolworth's in Greenboro, NC

- On February 1, 1960, four African American college students sat down at a lunch counter at Woolworth's in Greensboro, North Carolina, and politely asked for service. Their request was refused. When asked to leave, they remained in their seats. Their passive resistance and peaceful sit-down demand helped ignite a youth-led movement to challenge racial inequality throughout the South.

Most Powerful Earthquake Ever Recorded Hits Chile

- On this day in 1960, the first tremor of a series hits Valdivia, Chile. By the time they end, the quakes and their aftereffects kill 5,000 people and leave another 2 million homeless. Registering a magnitude of 7.6, the first earthquake was powerful and killed several people. It turned out to be only a foreshock, however, to one of the most powerful tremors ever recorded.

- At 3:11 p.m. the following afternoon, an 8.5-magnitude quake rocked southern Chile. The epicenter of this tremendous shaking was just off the coast under the Pacific Ocean. There, the Nazca oceanic plate plunged 50 feet down under the South American plate. The earthquake caused huge landslides of debris down the mountains of the region, as well as a series of tsunamis in the coastal region of Chile. At 4:20 p.m., a 26-foot wave hit the shore, taking most structures and buildings with it when it receded. But the worst was still to come. Minutes later, a slower 35-foot wave rolled in; it is estimated that this wave killed more than 1,000 people, including those who had thought they had moved safely to high ground.

Sharpeville Massacre in South Africa

- The Sharpeville massacre was a turning point in South African history. On March 21, 1960, without warning, South African police at Sharpeville, an African township of Vereeniging, south of Johannesburg, shot into a crowd of about 5,000 unarmed anti-pass protesters, killing at least 69 people – many of them shot in the back – and wounding more than 200.
- This massacre created a crisis for the apartheid government, both inside the country and internationally. The government immediately de-

clared a State of Emergency and banned political meetings. Within less than a month, it banned both the Pan Africanist Congress, which had organized the action in Sharpeville, and the African National Congress. After lengthy internal discussions, the ANC and PAC turned to armed struggle and went underground.
- News of the massacre drew immediate international condemnation. The South African stock exchange sank, saved only by loans from a consortium of U.S. banks.

The Birth Control Pill Is Approved by the FDA
- May 9, the Food and Drug Administration (FDA) approves the world's first commercially produced birth-control bill--Enovid-10, made by the G.D. Searle Company of Chicago, Illinois.

Walsh and Piccard Become the First to Explore the Deepest Place on Earth
- The voice of our faithful engineer, Giuseppe Buono, was taut with anxiety. A 37-year-old Italian, he had already prepared the Trieste for diving 64 times, first in the Mediterranean and this year in the western Pacific off Guam. Now he was wondering whether it was not sheer madness for the bathyscaph to attempt to descend 36,000 feet—nearly seven miles—under exist-

ing conditions. In fact, I was wondering the same thing myself.
- The date was January 23, 1960. The United States Navy's ocean-going tugboat Wandank had been towing the Trieste for four days; now we were some 220 miles from our base on Guam.

1961

Adolf Eichmann on Trial for Role in Holocaust
- After World War II, Nazi war criminal Adolf Eichmann fled from Austria and made his way to Argentina where he lived under the name Ricardo Klement. In May 1960, Israeli Security Service agents seized Eichmann in Argentina and took him to Jerusalem for trial in an Israeli court. Eichmann testified from a bulletproof glass booth.
- The Eichmann trial aroused international interest, bringing Nazi atrocities to the forefront of world news. Testimonies of Holocaust survivors, especially those of ghetto fighters such as Zivia Lubetkin, generated interest in Jewish resistance. The trial prompted a new openness in Israel; many Holocaust survivors felt able to share their experiences as the country confronted this traumatic chapter.

- Israeli attorney general Gideon Hausner signed a bill of indictment against Eichmann on 15 counts, including crimes against the Jewish people and crimes against humanity.
- The charges against Eichmann were numerous. After the Wannsee Conference (January 1942), Eichmann coordinated deportations of Jews from Germany and elsewhere in western, southern, and northern Europe to killing centers (through his representatives Alois Brunner, Theodor Dannecker, Rolf Guenther, and Dieter Wisliceny and others in the Gestapo). Eichmann made deportation plans down to the last detail. Working with other German agencies, he determined how the property of deported Jews would be seized and made certain that his office would benefit from the confiscated assets. He also arranged for the deportation of tens of thousands of Roma (Gypsies).
- Eichmann was also charged with membership in criminal organizations--the Storm Troopers (SA), Security Service (SD), and Gestapo (all of which had been declared criminal organizations at the 1946 Nuremberg Trial). As head of the Gestapo's section for Jewish affairs, Eichmann coordinated with Gestapo chief Heinrich Mueller on a plan to expel Jews from Greater Germany to Poland, which set the pattern for future deportations.

- For those and other charges, Eichmann was found guilty and sentenced to death. On June 1, 1962, Eichmann was executed by hanging. His body was cremated and the ashes were spread at sea, beyond Israel's territorial waters. The execution of Adolf Eichmann remains the only time that Israel has enacted a death sentence.

Bay of Pigs Invasion
- The Bay of Pigs invasion begins when a CIA-financed and -trained group of Cuban refugees lands in Cuba and attempts to topple the communist government of Fidel Castro. The attack was an utter failure.

Berlin Wall Built
- Two days after sealing off free passage between East and West Berlin with barbed wire, East German authorities begin building a wall--the Berlin Wall--to permanently close off access to the West. For the next 28 years, the heavily fortified Berlin Wall stood as the most tangible symbol of the Cold War--a literal "iron curtain" dividing Europe.

Freedom Riders Challenge Segregation on Interstate Buses
- On May 4, 1961, a group of 13 African-American and white civil rights activists

launched the Freedom Rides, a series of bus trips through the American South to protest segregation in interstate bus terminals. The Freedom Riders, who were recruited by the Congress of Racial Equality (CORE), a U.S. civil rights group, departed from Washington, D.C., and attempted to integrate facilities at bus terminals along the way into the Deep South. African-American Freedom Riders tried to use "whites-only" restrooms and lunch counters, and vice versa. The group encountered tremendous violence from white protestors along the route, but also drew international attention to their cause. Over the next few months, several hundred Freedom Riders engaged in similar actions. In September 1961, the Interstate Commerce Commission issued regulations prohibiting segregation in bus and train stations nationwide.

JFK Gives "Man on the Moon" Speech

- On May 25, 1961, President John F. Kennedy gave a historic speech before a joint session of Congress that set the United States on a course to the moon.
- In his speech, Kennedy called for an ambitious space exploration program that included not just missions to put astronauts on the moon, but

also a Rover nuclear rocket, weather satellites and other space projects.

Peace Corps Founded

- On March 1, 1961, President John F. Kennedy issues Executive Order #10924, establishing the Peace Corps as a new agency within the Department of State. The same day, he sent a message to Congress asking for permanent funding for the agency, which would send trained American men and women to foreign nations to assist in development efforts. The Peace Corps captured the imagination of the U.S. public, and during the week after its creation thousands of letters poured into Washington from young Americans hoping to volunteer.

Soviets Launch First Man in Space

- On April 12, 1961, aboard the spacecraft Vostok 1, Soviet cosmonaut Yuri Alekseyevich Gagarin becomes the first human being to travel into space. During the flight, the 27-year-old test pilot and industrial technician also became the first man to orbit the planet, a feat accomplished by his space capsule in 89 minutes. Vostok 1 orbited Earth at a maximum altitude of 187 miles and was guided entirely by an automatic control system. The only statement attributed to Gagarin during his one hour and 48 minutes in space was, "Flight is proceeding normally; I am well."

Stalin's Body Removed From Lenin's Mausoleum

- Five years after Soviet leader Nikita Khrushchev denounced Stalinism and the "personality cult" of Soviet rulers at the 20th Party Congress, Joseph Stalin's embalmed body is removed from Lenin's tomb in Moscow's Red Square.

The Antarctic Treaty Goes Into Force

- The Antarctic Treaty was signed in Washington on 1 December 1959 by the twelve countries whose scientists had been active in and around Antarctica during the International Geophysical Year (IGY) of 1957-58. It entered into force in 1961 and has since been acceded to by many other nations. The total number of Parties to the Treaty is now 50.

Tsar Bomba, the Largest Nuclear Weapon to Ever Be Exploded

- On October 23, 1961, Soviet pilot A. E. Durnovtsev guides his Tu-95 Bomber towards the Arctic Sea above Novaya Zemlya Island. This day will make atomic history, not as an advancement in nuclear science, but rather as a

statement of intimidation by the Soviet Union to the United States in those tense days now known as The Cold War.
- The bomber is carrying a secret cargo that will soon make the world take notice of Russia as a serious nuclear threat to the survival of mankind. For on this day a nuclear weapon rides into history as the largest thermonuclear bomb ever constructed and detonated named, "Tsar Bomba...King of the Bombs."

1962

Andy Warhol Exhibits His Campbell's Soup Can

- Andy Warhol's Campbell's Soup Cans transformed him into an overnight sensation when they were first exhibited in Los Angeles in 1962. It was his first one-person exhibition organized by Irving Blum, the legendary and visionary director of the Ferus Gallery. The exhibition featured thirty-two "portraits" of soup cans, each identical except for the flavor inscribed on their labels. These revolutionary paintings were displayed on a small narrow shelf that ran along the wall of the gallery in a way that suggested not only a gallery rail but also the long shelves in a grocery store. With these works, Warhol took on the tradition of still life painting, declaring a familiar household brand of packaged food a legitimate subject in the age of Post-War economic recovery.

Cuban Missile Crisis
- During the Cuban Missile Crisis, leaders of the U.S. and the Soviet Union engaged in a tense, 13-day political and military standoff in October 1962 over the installation of nuclear-armed Soviet missiles on Cuba, just 90 miles from U.S. shores. In a TV address on October 22, 1962, President John Kennedy (1917-63) notified Americans about the presence of the missiles, explained his decision to enact a naval blockade around Cuba and made it clear the U.S. was prepared to use military force if necessary to neutralize this perceived threat to national security. Following this news, many people feared the world was on the brink of nuclear war. However, disaster was avoided when the U.S. agreed to Soviet leader Nikita Khrushchev's (1894-1971) offer to remove the Cuban missiles in exchange for the U.S. promising not to invade Cuba. Kennedy also secretly agreed to remove U.S. missiles from Turkey.

Famous Escape From Alcatraz
- Over months of preparation, Morris and brothers John and Clarence Anglin removed the

air ventilation units in their cells, replaced them with fakes and made dummies to place in their beds to avoid tipping off guards. On the night of June 11, they slipped out through the vents and made it outside, then set off across San Francisco Bay on inflatable rafts fashioned from raincoats. They were never seen again, prompting claims that they were the only successful escapees in Alcatraz history. But pieces of a makeshift life vest and a bundle of letters wrapped in rubber were later found, suggesting that the men may have drowned amid the stiff currents and freezing waters of San Francisco Bay.
- In all, 36 men made a total of 14 escape attempts during Alcatraz's history. Of these, 23 were caught, six were shot and killed during their escape and two drowned. The remaining five (including Morris and the Anglins) went missing and were presumed drowned. The prison closed in March 1963 after operations became too expensive to continue, and the Rock is now part of the National Parks System.

First James Bond Movie
- The James Bond series focuses on a fictional character created in 1953 by writer Ian Fleming, who featured him in twelve novels and two short-story collections.

First Person Killed Trying to Cross the Berlin Wall

- On August 17, 1962, two young men from East Berlin attempted to scramble to freedom across the wall. One was successful in climbing the last barbed wire fence and, though suffering numerous cuts, made it safely to West Berlin. While horrified West German guards watched, the second young man was shot by machine guns on the East Berlin side. He fell but managed to stand up again, reach the wall, and begin to climb over. More shots rang out. The young man was hit in the back, screamed, and fell backwards off of the wall. For nearly an hour, he lay bleeding to death and crying for help. West German guards threw bandages to the man, and an angry crowd of West Berlin citizens screamed at the East German security men who seemed content to let the young man die. He finally did die, and East German guards scurried to where he lay and removed his body.

First Wal-Mart Opens

- Inspired by the early success of his dime store, and driven to bring even greater opportunity and value to his customers, Sam opened the first Walmart in 1962 at the age of 44 in

Rogers, Arkansas.

James Meredith Admitted Into the Segregated University of Mississippi
- James Howard Meredith (born June 25, 1933) is an American civil rights movement figure, a writer, and a political adviser. In 1962, he was the first African-American student admitted to the segregated University of Mississippi, an event that was a flashpoint in the American civil rights movement. Motivated by President John F. Kennedy's inaugural address, Meredith decided to exercise his constitutional rights and apply to the University of Mississippi. His goal was to put pressure on the Kennedy administration to enforce civil rights for African Americans.

Johnny Carson Takes Over the Tonight Show
- Oct 1,1962, Johnny Carson takes over from Jack Paar as host of the late-night talk program The Tonight Show. Carson went on to host The Tonight Show Starring Johnny Carson for three decades, becoming one of the biggest figures in entertainment in the 20th century.

Marilyn Monroe Found Dead
- Aug. 5, screen icon Marilyn Monroe has been found dead in bed at her Los Angeles home.

- The 36-year-old actress' body was discovered in the early hours of this morning by two doctors who were called to her Brentwood home by a concerned housekeeper.
- The doctors were forced to break into Miss Monroe's bedroom after being unable to open the door. She was found lying naked in her bed with an empty bottle of Nembutal sleeping pills by her side.
- The local coroner, who visited the scene later, said the circumstances of Miss Monroe's death indicated a "possible suicide".

Rachel Carson Publishes Silent Spring

- Silent Spring is an environmental science book written by Rachel Carson and published by Houghton Mifflin on September 27, 1962.[1] The book documented the detrimental effects of indiscriminate use of pesticides on the environment, particularly on birds. Carson accused the chemical industry of spreading disinformation, and public officials of accepting industry claims unquestioningly.

1963

16th Street Baptist Church Bombing

- Even as the inspiring words of Martin Luther King Jr.'s famous "I Have a Dream" speech rang out from the Lincoln Memorial during the historic March on Washington in August of 1963, racial relations in the segregated South were marked by continued violence and inequality. On September 15, a bomb exploded before Sunday morning services at the 16th Street Baptist Church in Birmingham, Alabama–a church with a predominantly black congregation that served as a meeting place for civil rights leaders. Four young girls were killed and many other people injured; outrage over the incident and the violent clash between protesters and police that followed helped draw national attention to the hard-fought, often dangerous struggle for civil rights for African Americans.

Betty Friedan Publishes The Feminine Mystique

- The publication of Betty Friedan's The Feminine Mystique, on February 17, 1963, is often cited as the founding moment of second-wave feminism. The book highlighted Friedan's view of a coercive and pervasive post-World War II ideology of female domesticity that stifled middle-class women's opportunities to be anything but homemakers.

Buddhist Monk Sets Himself on Fire in Protest

- Passers-by stop to watch as flames envelope a young Buddhist monk, Saigon, October 5th, 1963.
- The man sits impassively in the central market square, he has set himself on fire performing a ritual suicide in protest against governmental anti-Buddhist policies. Crowds gathered to protest in Hue after the South Vietnamese government prohibited Buddhists from carrying flags on Buddha's birthday. Government troops opened fire to disperse the dissidents, killing nine people, Diems government blamed the incident on the Vietcong and never admitted responsibility. The Buddhist leadership quickly organized demonstrations that eventually led to seven monks burning themselves to death.

First Dr. Who Episode Airs

- The very first episode was broadcast on Saturday 23rd November 1963. As this was the day immediately after the assassination of President Kennedy, the BBC, worried that not many people had seen the episode, decided to show it again the following Saturday, along with the second episode.

First Woman in Space
- On June 16, 1963, aboard Vostok 6, Soviet Cosmonaut Valentina Tereshkova becomes the first woman to travel into space. After 48 orbits and 71 hours, she returned to earth, having spent more time in space than all U.S. astronauts combined to that date.

Great Train Robbery in England
- The Great Train Robbery was the robbery of a Royal Mail train heading between Glasgow and London in the early hours of Thursday 8 August 1963 at Bridego Railway Bridge, Ledburn near Mentmore in Buckinghamshire, England.[2]
- After tampering with line signals, a 15-strong gang of robbers led by Bruce Reynolds attacked the train. Other gang members included Gordon Goody, Buster Edwards, Charlie Wilson, Roy James, John Daly, Jimmy White, Ronnie Biggs, Tommy Wisbey, Jim Hussey, Bob Welch and Roger Courdrey as well as three men known only as numbers '1', '2' and '3'. A 16th man, an unnamed retired train driver, was also present at the time of robbery.[3]
- With careful planning based on inside information from an individual known only as 'The Ulsterman', the robbers got away with over £2.6 million (the equivalent of £46 million today). The

bulk of the stolen money was never recovered. Though the gang did not use any firearms, Jack Mills, the train driver, was beaten over the head with a metal bar. Mills' injuries were severe enough to end his career.
- After the robbery the gang hid at Leatherslade Farm. It was after the police found this hideout that incriminating evidence would lead to the eventual arrest and conviction of most of the gang. The ringleaders were sentenced to 30 years in jail.

"Hot Line" Established Between U.S. and U.S.S.R.

- In June 1963, American and Russian representatives agreed to establish a so-called "hot line" between Moscow and Washington. The agreement came just months after the October 1962 Cuban missile crisis, in which the United States and Soviet Union came to the brink of nuclear conflict. It was hoped that speedier and more secure communications between the two nuclear superpowers would forestall such crises in the future. In August 1963, the system was ready to be tested. American teletype machines had been installed in the Kremlin to receive messages from Washington; Soviet teletypes were installed in the Pentagon. (Contrary to popular belief, the hot line in the United States is in the Pentagon, not the White House.) Both nations also exchanged encoding devices in order to decipher the messages. Messages from one nation to another would take just a matter of minutes, although the messages would then have to be translated. The messages would be carried by a 10,000-mile long cable connection, with "scramblers" along the way to insure that the messages could not be intercepted and read by unauthorized personnel. On August 30, the United States sent its first message to the Soviet Union over the hot line: "The quick brown fox jumped over the lazy dog's back 1234567890." The message used every letter and number key on the teletype machine in order to see that each was in working order. The return message from Moscow was in Russian, but it indicated that all of the keys on the Soviet teletype were also functioning.

- The hot line was never really necessary to prevent war between the Soviet Union and the United States, but it did provide a useful prop for movies about nuclear disaster, such as Fail Safe and Dr. Strangelove. Its significance at the time was largely symbolic. The two superpowers, who had been so close to mutual nuclear destruction in October 1962, clearly recognized the dangers of miscommunication or no communication in the modern world.

- Though the Cold War is over, the hot line continues in operation between the United States and Russia. It was supplemented in 1999 by a direct secure telephone connection between the two governments.

JFK Assassinated

- John Fitzgerald Kennedy, the 35th President of the United States, was assassinated at 12:30 p.m. Central Standard Time (18:30 UTC) on Friday, November 22, 1963, in Dealey Plaza, Dallas, Texas.[1][2] Kennedy was fatally shot by a sniper while traveling with his wife Jacqueline, Texas Governor John Connally, and Connally's wife Nellie, in a presidential motorcade. A ten-month investigation from November 1963 to September 1964 by the Warren Commission concluded that Kennedy was assassinated by Lee Harvey Oswald, acting alone, and that Jack Ruby also acted alone when he killed Oswald before he could stand trial.
- Although the Commission's conclusions were initially supported by a majority of the American public,[3] polls conducted between 1966 and 2003 found that as many as 80 percent of Americans have suspected that there was a plot or cover-up. A 1998 CBS News poll showed that 76% of Americans believed the President had been killed as the result of a conspiracy. A 2013

AP poll showed, that although the percentage had fallen, more than 59% of those polled still believed that more than one person was involved in the President's murder.[7][8] A Gallup Poll in mid-November 2013 showed 61% believed in a conspiracy and 30% thought Oswald did it alone.

March on Washington
- The March on Washington for Jobs and Freedom took place in Washington, D.C., on August 28, 1963. Attended by some 250,000 people, it was the largest demonstration ever seen in the nation's capital, and one of the first to have extensive television coverage.

Martin Luther King Jr. Makes His "I Have a Dream" Speech
- Martin Luther King's famous "I Have a Dream" speech, delivered at the 28 August 1963 March on Washington for Jobs and Freedom,

Medgar Evers Is Murdered
- June 12, in the driveway outside his home in Jackson, Mississippi, African American civil rights leader Medgar Evers is shot to death by white supremacist Byron De La Beckwith.

1964

Beatles Become Popular in U.S.

- Although Beatlemania had overtaken Great Britain, the Beatles still had the challenge of the United States. Despite already having achieved one number-one hit in the U.S. and had been greeted by 5,000 screaming fans when they arrived at the New York airport, it was the Beatles' February 9, 1964, appearance on The Ed Sullivan Show that ensured Beatlemania in America.

Cassius Clay (a.k.a. Muhammad Ali) Becomes World Heavyweight Champion

- Cassius Clay (a.k.a. Muhammad Ali) Becomes World Heavyweight Champion (1964): On February 25, 1964, Muhammad Ali, then still known as Cassius Clay, fought Charles "Sonny" Liston for the world heavyweight title in Miami, Florida.
- Liston expected an early knockout. However, Muhammad Ali was a lot faster than most other boxers. Ali's plan was to dance around the powerful Liston until Liston tired out. Ali's plan worked.
- By the 6th round, Liston was exhausted. He had also hurt his shoulder and was worried about a cut under his eye. When the bell for round seven rang, Liston shocked everyone when he re-

fused to continue the fight. Muhammad Ali was declared the winner and became the heavyweight boxing champion of the world.

Civil Rights Act Passes in U.S.
• The Civil Rights Act of 1964 (Pub.L. 88–352, 78 Stat. 241, enacted July 2, 1964) is a landmark piece of civil rights legislation in the United States[4] that outlawed discrimination based on race, color, religion, sex, or national origin.[5] It ended unequal application of voter registration requirements and racial segregation in schools, at the workplace and by facilities that served the general public (known as "public accommodations").

Hasbro Launches GI Joe Action Figure
• The action figure G.I. Joe was created by the Hasbro toy company in 1964, in part as a response to the popularity of Barbie dolls with American girls. Joe was a World War II-style fighting man, nearly 12 inches tall, and his movable joints -- right down to the wrists -- made him a fast hit with young boys.

Italy Asks for Help to Stabilize the Leaning Tower of Pisa
• On February 27, 1964, the Italian government announces that it is accepting suggestions

on how to save the renowned Leaning Tower of Pisa from collapse. The top of the 180-foot tower was hanging 17 feet south of the base, and studies showed that the tilt was increasing by a fraction every year. Experts warned that the medieval building--one of Italy's top tourist attractions--was in serious danger of toppling in an earthquake or storm. Proposals to save the Leaning Tower arrived in Pisa from all over the world, but it was not until 1999 that successful restorative work began.

Japan's First Bullet Train Line Opens
- It was the Japanese bullet train, however, that introduced modern high-speed rail services to the world in 1964. The dramatic appearance of its successive generations and association with technological excellence has made the bullet train synonymous with its homeland.

Nelson Mandela Sentenced to Life in Prison
- On June 12, 1964, Nelson Mandela received a life sentence for committing sabotage against South Africa's apartheid government, avoiding a possible death sentence.

Warren Report on JFK's Assassination Issued
- In its 888-page report presented to Johnson on September 24, 1964 (and released to

the public three days later), the commission concluded that the bullets that killed Kennedy and injured Connally were fired by Oswald in three shots from a rifle pointed out of a sixth-floor window in the Texas School Book Depository. Oswald's life, including a visit he made to the Soviet Union, was described in detail, but the report made no attempt to analyze his motives. Additionally, the commission found that the Secret Service had made poor preparations for Kennedy's visit to Dallas and had failed to sufficiently protect him, and concluded that Ruby had acted alone in killing Oswald.

1965

British Sea Gem Oil Rig Collapses
- In the autumn of 1965, the crew of the Sea Gem were drilling well 48/06- 1, which discovered gas in the Rotliegend Group sandstones. The well was completed on 09 December 1965 with tests indicating substantial gas reserves. At around 1345 hours on 27 December 1965, the crew were preparing to move the rig to a new location and commenced jacking down the main deck. A short time later, the passing freighter Baltrover witnessed the main deck lurch then fall towards port. The boat radioed for assistance at 1409 hours before coming to the aid

of the Sea Gem's crew. Two of the rig's ten legs had apparently failed, causing the rig to fall sideways. Survivors stated that after about thirty minutes, the rig subsequently capsized and sank with one leg remaining above the sea.

Los Angeles Riots
- On Wednesday, 11 August 1965, Marquette Frye, a 21-year-old black man, was arrested for drunk driving on the edge of Los Angeles' Watts neighborhood. The ensuing struggle during his arrest sparked off 6 days of rioting, resulting in 34 deaths, over 1,000 injuries, nearly 4,000 arrests, and the destruction of property valued at $40 million. On 17 August 1965, Martin Luther King arrived in Los Angeles in the aftermath of the riots.

Malcolm X Assassinated
- On February 21, in New York City, Malcolm X, an African American nationalist and religious leader, is assassinated by rival Black Muslims while addressing his Organization of Afro-American Unity at the Audubon Ballroom in Washington Heights.

Miniskirt First Appears
- The so-called mini-skirt is a skirt with a hemline well above the knees that is generally

no longer than 4 inches (10 cm) below the buttocks. In the olden days it was not usual, even a scandal if you attempted to show more legs then you should. Therefore short skirts were only seen in sport clothing, such as skirts worn by female tennis players. Unexpectedly fashion designer Mary Quant caused a modern revolution by inventing the first mini-skirt in the 'Swinging Sixties'. Already in the 1950s she began experimenting with shorter skirts for her own London boutique 'Baazar', while in 1965 her breakthrough came. Mary Quant finally accomplished freeing the women's world from conservative fashion with her invention after postwar period.

Nicolae Ceausescu Comes to Power in Romania

- Nicolae Ceaușescu (Romanian pronunciation: [nikoˈla.e t͡ʃea.uˈʃesku]; 26 January 1918 – 25 December 1989) was a Romanian communist politician. He was General Secretary of the Romanian Communist Party from 1965 to 1989, and as such was the country's last Communist leader. He was also the country's head of state from 1967 to 1989.
- A member of the Romanian Communist youth movement, Ceaușescu rose up through the ranks of Gheorghe Gheorghiu-Dej's Socialist government and, upon the death of Gheorghiu-

Dej in 1965, he succeeded to the leadership of Romania's Communist Party as General Secretary.

New York City Great Blackout
- Nov. 9, at dusk, the biggest power failure in U.S. history occurs as all of New York state, portions of seven neighboring states, and parts of eastern Canada are plunged into darkness. The Great Northeast Blackout began at the height of rush hour, delaying millions of commuters, trapping 800,000 people in New York's subways, and stranding thousands more in office buildings, elevators, and trains. Ten thousand National Guardsmen and 5,000 off-duty policemen were called into service to prevent looting.

The Rolling Stones' Mega Hit Song, "(I Can't Get No) Satisfaction"
- (I Can't Get No) Satisfaction is a hit riff-driven rock song written by Mick Jagger and Keith Richards for The Rolling Stones and produced by Andrew Loog Oldham. Rolling Stone magazine ranked the song as number 2 on its 500 Greatest Songs of All Time, while VH1 placed it at number 1 on its "100 Greatest Songs of Rock & Roll" list. In 2006 it was added to the Library of Congress National Recording Registry.

U.S. Sends Troops to Vietnam

- U.S. Sends Troops to Vietnam (1965): In response to the Gulf of Tonkin Incident of August 2 and 4, 1964, President Lyndon B. Johnson, per the authority given to him by Congress in the subsequent Gulf of Tonkin Resolution, decided to escalate the Vietnam Conflict by sending U.S. ground troops to Vietnam. On March 8, 1965, 3,500 U.S. Marines landed near Da Nang in South Vietnam; they are the first U.S. troops to arrive in Vietnam.

1966

Nazi Albert Speer Released From Spandau Prison

- Speer was released from prison on October 1st 1966. His autobiography became an international best-seller. While it gave a fascinating insight into the leaders of Nazi Germany, some felt that the book avoided the important issue of just how much Speer was a war criminal.

Black Panther Party Established

- In October of 1966, in Oakland California, Huey Newton and Bobby Seale founded the Black Panther Party for Self-Defense. The Panthers practiced militant self-defense of minority communities against the U.S. government, and fought to establish revolutionary socialism through mass organizing and community based programs.

First Kwanzaa Celebrated
- Kwanzaa is a week-long holiday honoring African culture and traditions. It falls between December 26 and January 1 each year. Maulana Karenga, an African-American leader, proposed this observance and it was first celebrated between December 1966 and January 1967.

Mao Zedong Launches the Cultural Revolution
- In 1966, China's Communist leader Mao Zedong launched what became known as the Cultural Revolution in order to reassert his authority over the Chinese government. Believing that current Communist leaders were taking the party, and China itself, in the wrong direction, Mao called on the nation's youth to purge the "impure" elements of Chinese society and revive the revolutionary spirit that had led to victory in the civil war 20 decades earlier and the formation of the People's Republic of China. The Cultural Revolution continued in various phases until Mao's death in 1976, and its tormented and

violent legacy would resonate in Chinese politics and society for decades to come.

Mass Draft Protests in U.S.
- Demonstrations grew in 1966, spurred by a change in the Selective Service System's draft policy that exposed students in the bottom of half of their classes to the possibility that their deferments would be revoked and they would be drafted. Teach-ins changed to sit-ins -- student take-overs of administration offices. A three-day event at the University of Chicago got national attention in May 1966, and University of Wisconsin students also staged their own occupation of an administration building that month.

National Organization for Women (NOW) Founded
- Oct. 29, - We, men and women who hereby constitute ourselves as the National Organization for Women, believe that the time has come for a new movement toward true equality for all women in America, and toward a fully equal partnership of the sexes, as part of the worldwide revolution of human rights now taking place within and beyond our national borders.

Star Trek T.V. Series Airs
- The first series, now referred to as "The Original Series", debuted in 1966 and ran for three seasons on NBC. It followed the interstellar adventures of James T. Kirk and the crew of the Starship Enterprise, an exploration vessel of a 23rd-century galactic "United Federation of Planets".

Two Multi-Ton Chunks of the Mundrabilla Meteorite Found
- Millions of years ago, a massive iron meteorite landed in Western Australia. Small chunks were found in 1911, but in 1966 two multi-ton pieces were discovered. These were named the Mundrabilla meteorite after the area where they were found.

1967

Australian Prime Minister Disappears
- Harold Edward Holt, CH (/hoʊlt/;[1] 5 August 1908 – 17 December 1967), was an Australian politician and the 17th Prime Minister of Australia.
- Holt spent 32 years in Parliament, including many years as a senior Cabinet Minister, but was Prime Minister for only 22 months. This abbreviated term necessarily limited his personal

and political impact, especially when compared to his immediate predecessor Sir Robert Menzies, who was Prime Minister for a total of 18 years.

Che Guevara Killed
- Guevara left Cuba in 1965 to foment revolution abroad, first unsuccessfully in Congo-Kinshasa and later in Bolivia, where he was captured by CIA-assisted Bolivian forces and summarily executed.

First Super Bowl
- The First AFL-NFL World Championship Game in professional American football, later known as Super Bowl I and referred to in some contemporary reports as the Supergame, was played on January 15, 1967 at the Los Angeles Memorial Coliseum in Los Angeles, California. The National Football League (NFL) champion Green Bay Packers defeated the American Football League (AFL) champion Kansas City Chiefs by the score of 35–10.

Six-Day War in the Middle East
- The Six-Day War took place in June 1967. The Six-Day War was fought between June 5th and June 10th. The Israelis defended the war as a preventative military effort to counter what the

Israelis saw as an impending attack by Arab nations that surrounded Israel. The Six-Day War was initiated by General Moshe Dayan, the Israeli's Defense Minister.

Stalin's Daughter Defects

- The death of Stalin's only daughter, Svetlana Alliluyeva, known as Lana Peters, made news around the world in November 2011. Svetlana was in the public eye ever since the spring of 1967, because of her decision to defect to the US. This caused a stir inside the Soviet leadership in the same year that the USSR was celebrating the 50th anniversary of the Great October Socialist Revolution. Although the international media published weeks on end articles on the subject of Svetlana's defection, the Soviet press declined to take a stand on the matter. However, a document from the archives of the ex-Romanian Communist Party shows very clearly the Kremlin's take on Svetlana's fleeing.

Three U.S. Astronauts Killed During Simulated Launch

- On Jan. 27, a launch pad fire during Apollo program tests at Cape Canaveral, Florida, kills astronauts Virgil "Gus" Grissom, Edward H. White II, and Roger B. Chafee. An investigation indicated that a faulty electrical wire inside the Apollo 1 command module was the probable cause of the fire. The astronauts, the first Americans to die in a spacecraft, had been participating in a simulation of the Apollo 1 launch scheduled for the next month.

Thurgood Marshall Becomes the First African-American U.S. Supreme Court Justice

- Aug. 30, 1967, Thurgood Marshall becomes the first African American to be confirmed as a Supreme Court justice. He would remain on the Supreme Court for 24 years before retiring for health reasons, leaving a legacy of upholding the rights of the individual as guaranteed by the U.S. Constitution.

1968

Japan's 300 Million Yen Robbery

- In 1968, a small bank in Japan began receiving threats that somebody was going to bomb the bank manager's house unless the blackmailer was paid ¥300,000,000. The police went to the house to guard it on the day it was supposed to be bombed, but the threat came and went and nothing happened.
- A few days later, a bank car carrying almost ¥300,000,000 (or about $800,000) was out to

deliver the money as bonuses . Normally, this car would only have two people accompanying the money, but because of all the recent threats, four people were in the car, guarding the money.

- As the car was rolling along, the four people in the van saw a uniformed man in the road signalling them to pull over. Assuming he was a police officer, they pulled over and rolled down their window.
- The man told the four bank employees that the bank manager's house had just been blown up, and that their car was the next target. Knowing that the bank manager had been threatened earlier that week, the four employees panicked and got out of the car.
- The uniformed man looked under the car and suddenly smoke and flames emerged. The employees ran and took cover and as they did, the uniformed man jumped into the car and drove away.
- The employees emerged, bewildered, to discover that they'd been tricked with a smoke bomb and flare. They also later found out that the bank manager's house hadn't, in fact, been blown up. The whole thing was a hoax, and the mysterious uniformed man walked away with a cool ¥300,000,000.

- And like that, ¥300,000,000 was gone. Nobody had been hurt, the crime had taken place in broad daylight, and the perpetrator disappeared without a trace. You could say that the thief was Japan's very own D. B. Cooper.

Martin Luther King Jr. Assassinated
- At 6:05 P.M. on Thursday, 4 April 1968, Martin Luther King was shot dead while standing on a balcony outside his second-floor room at the Lorraine Motel in Memphis, Tennessee. News of King's assassination prompted major outbreaks of racial violence, resulting in more than 40 deaths nationwide and extensive property damage in over 100 American cities. James Earl Ray, a 40-year-old escaped fugitive, later confessed to the crime and was sentenced to a 99-year prison term. During King's funeral a tape recording was played in which King spoke of how he wanted to be remembered after his death: "I'd like somebody to mention that day that Martin Luther King Jr. tried to give his life serving others"

My Lai Massacre
- The My Lai massacre is probably one of the most infamous events of the Vietnam War.

The My Lai massacre took place on March 16th 1968.
- My Lai was a village of about 700 inhabitants some 100 miles to the southeast of the US base of Danang. Shortly after dawn on March 16th, three platoons of US troops from C Company, 11th Brigade, arrived in the Son My area having been dropped off by helicopters. 1 Platoon was commanded by Lieutenant William Calley and was ordered to My Lai village. They were part of Task Force Barker – the codename for a search and destroy mission. They had been told to expect to find members of the NLF (called Vietcong or VC by the US soldiers) in the vicinity as the village was in an area where the NLF had been very active.
- When the troops from 1 Platoon moved through the village they started to fire at the villagers. These were women, children and the elderly as the young men had gone to the paddy fields to work. Sergeant Michael Bernhardt, who was at My Lai, was quoted in 1973 as stating that he saw no one who could have been considered to be of military age. He also stated that the US troops in My Lai met no resistance. An army photographer, Ronald Haeberie, witnessed a US soldier shoot two young boys who he believed were no more than five years of age. Other photos taken at the scene of the mas-

sacre show bodies of what can only be very young children.
- Those who returned to the village claimed that it took three days to bury the bodies. They were later to report that some of the children had their throats cut and that some of the bodies had not just been shot but had also been mutilated.

- What happened at My Lai only came to public light in November 1969 when a US soldier, Paul Meadlo, was interviewed on television and admitted killing "ten of fifteen men, women and children" at My Lai. His admission caused much shock and a great deal of pressure was put on the US military to launch an investigation. In fact, the US military was already aware of the allegations and had launched an investigation in April 1969, some six months before the public was made aware of what had gone on. It soon became clear that many hundreds of villagers had been killed. The actual number killed was never established but it was officially put as no less than 175 while it could have been as high as 504. The two most common figures put on casualties are 347 and 504. The memorial at My Lai itself lists 504 names with ages that range from one to eighty-two years. An official US army investigation came out with the figure of 347.

- Though a number of US soldiers were charged, all with the exception of Lieutenant William Calley, were acquitted. Calley was sentenced to life in prison with hard labour. He served three years before he was released. However, Calley had his supporters and many believed that he was simply following orders. His defence, which was initially rejected, was that he was there in My Lai to hunt out communists and to destroy communism and that he was only carrying out his orders that were to hunt out the NLF. 'The Battle Hymn of William Calley', a record in support of Calley, sold over 200,000 copies.

Nerve Gas Leak in Utah Kills 6,000 Sheep
- The weather was far from optimal on March 13, 1968. There were ominous thunderheads and shifting winds. It was not the best day to play with nerve gas, but a bunch of VIPs were visiting Utah's Dugway Proving Grounds and the Dugway crew was eager to show off. A Phantom jet loaded with more than a ton of nerve agent in a spray tank closed in on its target and expelled its load. And then some. Apparently, a valve didn't close and about 20 pounds of VX agent was inadvertently sprayed beyond the target zone. Soon after, about 30 miles away in Skull Valley, sheep started to convulse and die. Over the next few days, more

than 6,000 sheep sickened, dropped, shuddered and expired.
- The Army denied any responsibility, though they eventually compensated the sheep owners for their loss. Today, they still deny responsibility. Data on the sheep, they say, is "inconclusive." But a recently discovered Army document says otherwise. According to the Salt Lake Tribune, the report confirms that traces of VX were found in the death zone. Added to other reports showing chemical indications of nerve agent in body samples from the dead sheep, the new evidence closes the case on the Army's responsibility.

Prague Spring
- The Prague Spring of 1968 is the term used for the brief period of time when the government of Czechoslovakia led by Alexander Dubček seemingly wanted to democratise the nation and lessen the stranglehold Moscow had on the nation's affairs. The Prague Spring ended with a Soviet invasion, the removal of Alexander Dubček as party leader and an end to reform within Czechoslovakia.

Robert F. Kennedy Assassinated
- Shortly after midnight on June 5, 1968, presidential candidate Robert F. Kennedy was

shot three times by Palestinian immigrant Sirhan Sirhan after giving a speech at the Ambassador Hotel in Los Angeles, California. Robert Kennedy died of his wounds 26 hours later. Robert Kennedy's assassination later led to Secret Service protection for all future major presidential candidates.

Spy Ship USS Pueblo Captured

- On January 23, 1968, the USS Pueblo, a Navy intelligence vessel, is engaged in a routine surveillance of the North Korean coast when it is intercepted by North Korean patrol boats. According to U.S. reports, the Pueblo was in international waters almost 16 miles from shore, but the North Koreans turned their guns on the lightly armed vessel and demanded its surrender. The Americans attempted to escape, and the North Koreans opened fire, wounding the commander and two others. With capture inevitable, the Americans stalled for time, destroying the classified information aboard while taking further fire. Several more crew members were wounded.

Tet Offensive

- On January 31, 1968, some 70,000 North Vietnamese and Viet Cong forces launched the Tet Offensive (named for the lunar new year holiday called Tet), a coordinated series of fierce attacks on more than 100 cities and towns in South Vietnam. General Vo Nguyen Giap, leader of the Communist People's Army of Vietnam (PAVN), planned the offensive in an attempt both to foment rebellion among the South Vietnamese population and encourage the United States to scale back its support of the Saigon regime. Though U.S. and South Vietnamese forces managed to hold off the Communist attacks, news coverage of the offensive (including the lengthy Battle of Hue) shocked and dismayed the American public and further eroded support for the war effort. Despite heavy casualties, North Vietnam achieved a strategic victory with the Tet Offensive, as the attacks marked a turning point in the Vietnam War and the beginning of the slow, painful American withdrawal from the region.

Zodiac Killer Strikes

- The Zodiac Killer was a serial killer who operated in northern California in the late 1960s and early 1970s. The killer's identity remains unknown. The Zodiac murdered victims in Benicia, Vallejo, Lake Berryessa, and San Francisco between December 1968 and October 1969. Four men and three women between the ages of 16 and 29 were targeted. The killer originated the name "Zodiac" in a series of taunting letters sent to the local Bay Area press. These letters included four cryptograms (or ciphers). Of the four cryptograms sent, only one has been definitively solved.

1969

Manson Family Murders
- According to the book Helter Skelter – The True Story Of the Manson Murders by Vincent Bugliosi (lead prosecutor of the case) and Curt Gentry, Charles Manson directed Charles Watson, Susan Atkins, Linda Kasabian, and Patricia Krenwinkel to enter the Tate residence (formerly the Melcher residence, who rejected Mason's music compilation) and to "destroy everyone in it – as gruesome as you can." Watson, Atkins, Kasabian, and Krenwinkel all climbed up a brushy platform to gain entrance into the property. While they were trespassing, Steven Parent, a visitor of the residence's caretaker, William Garretson, was leaving the property in his vehicle. Watson stopped Parent, swung a knife at him, and then shot him four times in the chest and abdomen.
- Watson entered the residence by cutting the screen of a window and opened the front door for Atkins and Krenwinkel. Kasabian was at the

end of the driveway to "keep watch." Watson and the group entered the residence and found Tate, Folger, Frykowski, and Sebring. Tate and Sebring were tied together by their necks and Folger was taken into a nearby bedroom. Sebring was shot and stabbed seven times. Frykowski was bound by a towel but managed to free himself. After doing so, he became involved in a physical altercation with Atkins resulting in her stabbing him in the legs. Frykowski continued to flee but Watson struck him with the gun multiple times over the head, shot, and stabbed him multiple times. The gun grip broke off as a result of Watson striking Frykowski over the head.

- Folger fled the room she was taken to and then was chased by Krenwinkel. Folger was initially stabbed by Krenwinkel but soon after was being stabbed by Watson as well. Folger was stabbed a total of 28 times by both Krenwinkel and Watson. While this was occurring, Frykowski was struggling across the lawn when Watson came to stab him again. Frykowski was stabbed a total of 51 times.
- Tate, witnessing the horrific crimes, pleaded with Atkins for mercy but was rejected. Tate was stabbed a total of 16 times. Tate's unborn child did not survive the incident.

LaBianca Murder

- On August 10, 1969, the night after the Tate murder, Manson and six of the Manson family members (Leslie Van Houten, Steve Grogan, Susan Atkins, Linda Kasabian, Patricia Krenwinkel, and Charles Watson)joined in on another murder. Unlike the Tate murder, Manson joined in on the LaBianca murder beause he felt that there was not enough panic among the victims from the Tate murder. Manson and the family members drove around for prospective murder victims when they arrived in the neighborhood of a home in which they had attended a party a year prior. The neighboring home belonged to a successful Grocery company owner, Leno LaBianca, and his wife, Rosemary LaBianca.
- Due to the several differing accounts of Manson and the six Manson family members, the exact happenings of the murder are not certain. Manson claims that he approached the home alone and returned later to bring Watson along. When Manson and Watson were in the residence, they tied up the LaBianca couple with a lamp cord and with pillowcases covering their heads. Manson reassured the couple that they would not be hurt and that they were being robbed. All the cash was collected and the bounded Rosemary

was returned to her room. Soon after, Van Houten and Krenwinkel entered the premises with the instructions from Manson to kill the couple. Manson left the residence and instructed Van Houten and Krenwinkel to follow Watson's orders.
- Watson began stabbing Leno multiple times when Leno cried out to stop stabbing him. Afterwards in the bedroom, Rosemary began to swing the lamp still attached to cord wrapped around her neck. Van Houten and Krenwinkel yelled for Watson's aid and stabbed Rosemary multiple times. Watson gave the knife to Van Houten and she continued to stab Rosemary. Rosemary was stabbed a total of 41 times by Watson, Van Houten, and Krenwinkel.
- Watson returned to the living room and continued to stab and kill Leno. Krenwinkel carved the word "WAR" into Leno's stomach, stabbed Leno multiple times, left a carving fork sticking out from his stomach, and left a knife in Leno's throat. Leno was stabbed a total of 26 times.
- On the walls of the living room, "Death to pigs" and "Rise" were written in Leno's blood. On the refrigerator door, a misspelled "Healter [sic] Skelter" was smeared.

Neil Armstrong Becomes the First Man on the Moon

- Historical Importance of the First Man on the Moon: For thousands of years, man had looked to the heavens and dreamed of walking on the moon. In 1969, as part of the Apollo 11 mission, Neil Armstrong became the very first to accomplish that dream, followed only minutes later by Buzz Aldrin. Their accomplishment placed the United States ahead of the Soviets in the Space Race and gave people around the world the hope of future space exploration.

Rock-and-Roll Concert at Woodstock
- The Woodstock Festival was a three-day concert (which rolled into a fourth day) that involved lots of sex, drugs, and rock 'n roll - plus a lot of mud. The Woodstock Music Festival of 1969 has become an icon of the 1960s hippie counterculture.

Senator Edward Kennedy Leaves the Scene of an Accident
- Around midnight on the night of July 18-19, 1969, U.S. Senator Ted Kennedy had left a party and was driving his black, Oldsmobile sedan when it went off a bridge and landed in Poucha Pond on Chappaquiddick Island, Massachusetts. Kennedy survived the accident but his passenger, 28-year-old Mary Jo Kopechne,

did not. Kennedy fled the scene and did not report the accident for nearly ten hours.
- Although Ted Kennedy was subjected to a subsequent investigation and proceedings, he was not charged with causing Kopechne's death; a point that many contend was a direct result of Kennedy family connections. The Chappaquiddick incident remained a scar on Ted Kennedy's reputation and thus prevented him from making a serious run at becoming president of the United States.

Sesame Street First Airs
- Nov. 10, 1969, "Sesame Street," a pioneering TV show that would teach generations of young children the alphabet and how to count, makes its broadcast debut. "Sesame Street," with its memorable theme song ("Can you tell me how to get/How to get to Sesame Street"), went on to become the most widely viewed children's program in the world. It has aired in more than 120 countries.

Yasser Arafat Becomes Leader of the PLO
- Arafat helped found Al Fatah in 1959 and in 1965 returned to Egypt to head Al Assifa, the military arm of Al Fatah. He went on to become leader of Al Fatah, and when the group gained control of the PLO (1969), Arafat was named

Inventions & Events

the larger body's chairman. The PLO won wide support among Palestinians and third-world nations during the 1970s and 80s, although it was weakened by internal divisions. In 1983, after an Israeli invasion of Lebanon, the PLO was forced to move its headquarters to Tunisia.

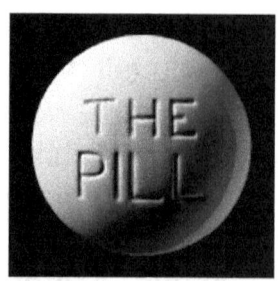

The 60's were indeed a busy year. Many inventions and many events. These are only some of the accomplishments that happened in the 60's.

Inventions & Events

Nixon 68-74   Ford 74-76   Carter 76-80

1970 - 1979 - Inventions

1970

The daisy-wheel printer invented.
- A Daisy Wheel Printer is an old fashioned impact printer, based on electric typewriter technology. All of the characters (letters, numbers, and punctuation marks) were on spokes radiating from a central axle and somewhat resembled a daisy, hence the name. The printing was relatively slow, but the impressions were incredibly clear as long as there was a fresh printer ribbon.

The floppy disk invented by Alan Shugart.
- The first floppy was an 8-inch flexible plastic disk coated with magnetic iron oxide;

computer data was written to and read from the disk's surface.
- The nickname "floppy" came from the disk's flexibility. The floppy disk was considered a revolutionary device in the "History of Computers" for its portability which provided a new and easy physical means of transporting data from computer to computer.

1971

The dot-matrix printer invented.
- The term DOT matrix refers to the process of placing dots to form an image; the quality of the image being determined by the dots per inch.
- Dot matrix printerAlternatively referred to as a pin printer, Dot matrix printers were first introduced by Centronics in 1970 and is a printer that uses print heads to shoot ink or strike an ink ribbon to place hundreds to thousands of little dots to form text or images.

The food processor invented.
- The food processor was invented by a French catering company salesman in 1960. Pierre Verdon named his invention the Robot-Coupe. By 1971 this machine was renamed the Le Magi-Max. In 1973 Pierre Verdon met an

American inventor; Carl Sonthemier who refined the construction, design and look of Pierre's original food processor. The improvements were astonishing and they agreed to create a new name for this appliance that would prepare food in a fraction of the time manual preparation would take. This new food processor debuted in 1973 and was finally named the Cuisinart.

The liquid-crystal display (LCD) invented by James Fergason.

- The technology was patented in the United States by Fergason in 1971. Fergason formed his own company, ILIXCO, in 1968 to manufacture liquid crystal displays. His first customers were the Bulova Watch Company and Gruen Watch Company which used the technology to market the first LCD watches using this technology. By the end of the decade, most of the world's digital watches used this kind of LCD display.

The microprocessor invented by Faggin, Hoff and Mazor.

- Federico Faggin, currently CEO of Synaptics, led the design and development of the world's first microprocessor, the Intel 4004 and conceived and supervised the design of the

landmark 8080, the first modern microprocessor.
- In November, 1971, a company called Intel publicly introduced the world's first single chip microprocessor, the Intel 4004 (U.S. Patent #3,821,715), invented by Intel engineers Federico Faggin, Ted Hoff, and Stanley Mazor.

VCR or videocassette invented.
- The Video Home System (better known by its abbreviation VHS) is a consumer-level analog recording videotape-based cassette standard developed by Victor Company of Japan (JVC).
- The 1970s was a period when video recording became a major contributor to the television industry. Like many other technological innovations, each of several companies made an attempt to produce a television recording standard that the majority of the world would embrace. At the peak of it all, the home video industry was caught up in a series of videotape format wars. Two of the formats, VHS and Betamax, received the most media exposure. VHS would eventually win the war, and therefore succeed as the dominant home video format, lasting throughout the tape format period.
- In later years, optical disc formats began to offer better quality than video tape. The earliest of

these formats, Laserdisc, was not widely adopted, but the subsequent DVD format eventually did achieve mass acceptance and replaced VHS as the preferred method of distribution after 2000.

1972

The word processor invented.
- In 1972 Lexitron and Linolex developed a similar word processing system, but included video display screens and tape cassettes for storage. With the screen, text could be entered and corrected without having to produce a hard copy. Printing could be delayed until the writer was satisfied with the material.

Pong first video game invented by Nolan Bushnell.
- Pong was the invention of Nolan Bushnell, a young engineer who introduced video table tennis to arcades in 1972. Simple and addictive, Pong launched the craze for home video games. The home version was Introduced by Atari, Bushnell's company, in 1974--long before anyone had seen a personal computer.

Hacky Sack invented by John Stalberger and Mike Marshall.

- Hacky Sack or Footbag, as we know it today, is a modern American sport invented in 1972, by John Stalberger and Mike Marshall of Oregon City, Oregon. Marshall had created a hand-made bean bag, that he was kicking around. Stalberger was recovering from knee surgery and was looking for a fun way to exercise his knees. Together, they called the new game "Hackin' the Sack." The two decided to collaborate and market their new game under the trademark of "Hacky Sack®"

1973

Gene splicing invented.
- Herb Boyer and Stanley Cohen were the men who invented gene splicing in 1973. They placed a gene from a toad called a Xenopus into bacterial DNA. A year earlier a scientist named Paul Berg actually used gene splicing to create DNA molecules. He was actually the first scientist to splice together DNA strands from two different organisms together. His research made the discovery of restriction enzymes by Daniel Nathans and Hamilton Othanel Smith possible.

Inventions & Events

The ethernet (local computer network) invented by Robert Metcalfe and Xerox.
- The ethernet is a system for connecting computers within a building using hardware running from machine to machine. It differs from the Internet, which connects remotely located computers by telephone line, software protocol and some hardware. Ethernet uses some software (borrowed from Internet Protocol), but the connecting hardware was the basis of the patent (#4,063,220) involving newly designed chips and wiring. The patent* describes ethernet as a "multipoint data communication system with collision detection".

Bic invents the disposable lighter.
- In 1970 Gillette purchased the S. T. Dupont Company, a prestigious French manufacturer whose principal product was luxury cigarette lighters that sold for hundreds of dollars. During this time Dupont explored the possibilities of marketing a disposable lighter, developing an inexpensive disposable lighter called Cricket, which it introduced in the United States in 1972. Later that year Time reported that BIC was test marketing a disposable lighter that could provide 3,000 lights before wearing out. BIC introduced this lighter in 1973.

1974

The post-it notes invented by Arthur Fry.
- The Post It Note may have been a Godsent, literally. In the early 1970s, Art Fry was in search of a bookmark for his church hymnal that would neither fall out nor damage the hymnal. Fry noticed that a colleague at 3M, Doctor Spencer Silver, had developed an adhesive in 1968 that was strong enough to stick to surfaces, but left no residue after removal and could be repositioned. Arthur Fry took some of Spencer Silver's adhesive and applied it along the edge of a piece of paper. His church hymnal problem was solved!

Giorgio Fischer, a gynecologist from Rome, Italy, invents liposuction.
- Liposuction (or lipoplasty) is a technique in which excess fatty tissue is suctioned from beneath the skin. Prior to surgery, doctors flush the targeted area or areas with a solution composed of lidocaine (a local anesthetic similar in its numbing effects to novocaine), saline, and epinephrine (a drug that constricts blood vessels and thus reduces bleeding during surgery).
- Then doctors insert a hollow wand-like device called a cannula through incisions in the skin. They push and pull the cannula around through

fatty deposits, breaking up the cells, which, along with other body fluids, are suctioned out by an attached vacuuming device. There are several liposuction techniques available today. The amount of injected fluid determines the technique used.

1975

The laser printer invented.
- Gary Starkweather invented the laser printer while working a Xerox in 1969. Laser printers were not commercially available until IBM released a model in 1975. The first laser printers were so large they often took up an entire room.

The push-through tab on a drink can invented.
- The safety and litter problems were both eventually solved later in the 1970s with Ermal Fraze's invention of the non-removing "pop-tab". The pull-ring was replaced with a stiff aluminium lever, and the removable tab was replaced with a pre-scored round tab that functioned similarly to the push-tab, but the raised blister was no longer needed, as the riveted lever would now do the job of pushing the tab open and into the interior of the can.

1976

The ink-jet printer invented.
- It has been found that no one person can be credited with having invented the inkjet printer. Many different companies and participants worked together to create the inkjet printer. It is safe to say that the inkjet printer was first released in 1976 but did not become popular until 1988.

1977

Magnetic resonance imaging invented by Raymond V. Damadian.
- Magnetic resonance imaging or scanning (also called an MRI) is a method of looking inside the body without using surgery, harmful dyes or x-rays. The MRI scanner uses magnetism and radio waves to produce clear pictures of the human anatomy.

1978

Dan Bricklin and Bob Frankston invented the VisiCalc spreadsheet.
- VisiCalc was the first computer spreadsheet program. It was released to the public in 1979, running on an Apple II computer. While

most early microprocessor computers had been quickly supported by BASIC and a few games, VisiCalc introduced a new level in application software. It was considered a fourth generation software program. Companies invested time and money in doing financial projections with manually calculated spreadsheets, where changing a single number meant recalculating every single cell in the sheet. With VisiCalc, you could change any cell, and the entire sheet would be automatically recalculated.

The artificial heart Jarvik-7 invented by Robert K. Jarvik.
- Dr. Robert Jarvik is widely known as the inventor of the first permanent total artificial heart. In the mid-1970s, he and fellow researchers at the University of Utah designed and developed the air-driven Jarvik-7 total artificial heart, the first to successfully sustain a dying patient with the goal of lifelong support.

1979

Walkman invented.
- According to Sony, "In 1979, an empire in personal portable entertainment was created with the ingenious foresight of Sony Founder and Chief Advisor, the late Masaru Ibuka, and

Sony Founder and Honorary Chairman Akio Morita. It began with the invention of the first cassette Walkman TPS-L2 that forever changed the way consumers listen to music."

Scott Olson invents roller blades.
- Scott Olson and Brennan Olson, brothers and hockey players who lived in Minneapolis, Minnesota, found an antique pair of roller skates. It was one of the early skates that used the in-line wheels rather than the four-wheeled parallel design of George Plimpton. Intrigued by the in-line design, the brothers began redesigning roller skates, taking design elements from the found skates and using modern materials. They used polyurethane wheels, attached the skates to ice hockey boots, and added a rubber toe-brake to their new design.

I, purposely, didn't include all the inventions in the '70's, or any other year, since the world is spinning faster and faster it is hard to stay up with all the new things.

I have tried to vary the articles so it could remain interesting as well as informative.

1970 - 1979 Events

1970

Aswan High Dam Completed
- After 11 years of construction, the Aswan High Dam across the Nile River in Egypt is completed on July 21, 1970. More than two miles long at its crest, the massive $1 billion dam ended the cycle of flood and drought in the Nile River region, and exploited a tremendous source of renewable energy, but had a controversial environmental impact.
- A dam was completed at Aswan, 500 miles south of Cairo, in 1902. The first Aswan dam provided valuable irrigation during droughts but could not hold back the annual flood of the mighty Nile River. In the 1950s, Egyptian leader Gamal Abdel Nasser envisioned building a new dam across the Nile, one large enough to end flooding and bring electric power to every corner of Egypt. He won United States and British financial backing, but in July 1956 both nations canceled the offer after learning of a secret Egyptian arms agreement with the USSR. In response, Nasser nationalized the British and French-owned Suez Canal, intending to use tolls to pay for his High Dam project. This act

precipitated the Suez Canal Crisis, in which Israel, Britain, and France attacked Egypt in a joint military operation. The Suez Canal was occupied, but Soviet, U.S., and U.N. forced Israel, Britain, and France to withdraw, and the Suez Canal was left in Egyptian hands in 1957.

Beatles Break Up

- The break-up of the Beatles, one of the most popular and influential musical groups in history,[1] has become almost as much of a legend as the band itself or the music they created while together. The Beatles were active from their formation in 1960 to the disintegration of the group in 1970.

Palestinian Group Hijacks Five Planes

- Hijackers from Palestine armed with weapons hijack planes at European airports. They used passengers to bargin for the release of Palastinian Militants held in Europe and Israel. Hijackers told hosteges they would be killed unless governments of Great Britain, Switzerland, Germany and Israel agreed to release Palestinian prisoners.

Kent State Shootings

- On May 4, 1970 members of the Ohio National Guard fired into a crowd of Kent State

University demonstrators, killing four and wounding nine Kent State students. The impact of the shootings was dramatic. The event triggered a nationwide student strike that forced hundreds of colleges and universities to close. H. R. Haldeman, a top aide to President Richard Nixon, suggests the shootings had a direct impact on national politics. In The Ends of Power, Haldeman (1978) states that the shootings at Kent State began the slide into Watergate, eventually destroying the Nixon administration. Beyond the direct effects of the May 4th, the shootings have certainly come to symbolize the deep political and social divisions that so sharply divided the country during the Vietnam War era.

1971

London Bridge Brought to the U.S.
- Reconstructing the London Bridge in Lake Havasu City was done in the same manner as the Egyptians built pyramids. Sand mounds beneath each arch were carefully formed to the profile of the original bridge arches, serving the same function as molds. When work was completed the sand was removed. a one-mile channel was dredged and water was diverted from

the lake, under the Bridge, then back into the lake.
- The reconstructed London Bridge was dedicated in Lake Havasu City on October 10, 1971 with many British and Arizona officials participating in this event that drew 50,000 spectators.

United Kingdom Changes to Decimal System for Currency

- The British Government has launched a new decimal currency across the country.
- The familiar pound (£), shilling (s) and pence (d) coins are to be phased out over the next 18 months in favour of a system dividing the pound into units of ten, including half, one, two, five, ten and 50 pence denominations.
- Chairman of the Decimal Currency Board (DCB) Lord Fiske told reporters: "The general picture is quite clear and the smooth and efficient changeover so many people have worked for is now in fact being achieved."

VCRs Introduced

- Video Cassette Recording (VCR) is an early domestic analog recording format designed by Philips. It was the first successful consumer-level home videocassette recorder (VCR) system. Later variants included the VCR-LP and Super Video (SVR) formats.

- The VCR format was introduced in 1972, just after the Sony U-matic format in 1971. Although at first glance the two might appear to have been competing formats, they were aimed at very different markets. U-matic was introduced as a professional television production format, whilst VCR was targeted particularly at educational but also domestic users. Unlike some other early formats such as Cartrivision, the VCR format does record a high-quality video signal without resorting to Skip field.

1972

M*A*S*H T.V. Show Premiers
- M*A*S*H is an American television series developed by Larry Gelbart, adapted from the 1970 feature film MASH (which was itself based on the 1968 novel MASH: A Novel About Three Army Doctors, by Richard Hooker). The series, which was produced in association with 20th Century Fox Television for CBS, follows a team of doctors and support staff stationed at the "4077th Mobile Army Surgical Hospital" in Uijeongbu, South Korea during the Korean War. The show's title sequence features an instrumental version of "Suicide Is Painless", the theme song from the original film. The show was created after an attempt to film the original

book's sequel, M*A*S*H Goes to Maine, failed. The T.V show version of MASH is the most well known version of the M*A*S*H works, and one of the highest rated shows in U.S. television history.

Mark Spitz Wins Seven Gold Medals

- U.S. swimmer Mark Spitz wins his seventh gold medal at the 1972 Summer Olympics in Munich. Spitz swam the fly leg of the 400-meter medley relay, and his team set a new world-record time of 3 minutes, 48.16 seconds. Remarkably, Spitz also established new world records in the six other events in which he won the gold. At the time, no other athlete had won so many gold medals at a single Olympiad. The record would stand until Michael Phelps took home eight gold medals at the Beijing Games in 2012.

Pocket Calculators Introduced

- In the early 1970s, the daily lives of people throughout the developed world were changed profoundly by the advent of a small electronic machine that could per-form basic mathematical problems much more quickly and more accurately than they could be worked out on paper. Calculators expanded the math capabilities of everyone from high school students to businessmen.

Terrorists Attack at the Olympic Games in Munich

- Early in the morning on September 5, 1972, eight members of the Palestinian terrorist organization, Black September, snuck into the Olympic Village at the XXth Olympic Games which were held in Munich, Germany.
- The Black September members raided the building housing the Israeli athletes. Two Israeli athletes were killed during the raid and nine others were taken hostage.
- After spending most of the day trying to negotiate an exchange of prisoners for the hostages, the Black September members finally realized that their demands were not going to be met. They then asked for transport to an airport and two planes to take them to Cairo, Egypt.
- German officials decided that they could not let the terrorists leave the country with the hostages and so they prepared for a rescue attempt at the airport. Unfortunately, the rescue attempt failed and all nine of the Israeli hostages were killed during the shoot-out. Five of the Black September members were killed and the other three were taken into custody.

Watergate Scandal Begins

- The Watergate scandal was a major political scandal that occurred in the United States in the 1970s as a result of the June 17, 1972 break-in at the Democratic National Committee headquarters at the Watergate office complex in Washington, D.C., and the Nixon administration's attempted cover-up of its involvement. The term Watergate has come to encompass an array of clandestine and often illegal activities undertaken by members of the Nixon administration. Those activities included "dirty tricks" such as bugging the offices of political opponents and people of whom Nixon or his officials were suspicious. Nixon and his close aides ordered harassment of activist groups and political figures, using the FBI, CIA, and the Internal Revenue Service. The scandal led to the discovery of multiple abuses of power by the Nixon administration, articles of impeachment, and the resignation of Republican Richard Nixon, the President of the United States, on August 9, 1974—the only resignation of a U.S. president to date. The scandal also resulted in the indictment, trial, conviction, and incarceration of 43 people, dozens of whom were Nixon's top administration officials.

1973

Roe vs Wade Legalizes Abortion in the U.S.
- Roe v. Wade, 410 U.S. 113 (1973), is a landmark decision by the United States Supreme Court on the issue of abortion. Decided simultaneously with a companion case, Doe v. Bolton, the Court ruled 7–2 that a right to privacy under the due process clause of the 14th Amendment extended to a woman's decision to have an abortion, but that right must be balanced against the state's two legitimate interests in regulating abortions: protecting prenatal life and protecting women's health. Arguing that these state interests became stronger over the course of a pregnancy, the Court resolved this balancing test by tying state regulation of abortion to the trimester of pregnancy.

Paul Getty Kidnapped
- Getty initially became reclusive after the death of his second wife in 1971. He moved to Rome as head of Getty Oil Italiana. In 1973, his eldest son, John Paul Getty III, was kidnapped in Rome by Calabrian mobsters and held in the Calabrian Mountains, chained to a stake in a cave. Getty did not have enough money to pay the $17 million ransom demand, and his father refused to help, saying "I have 14 other grand-

children, and if I pay one penny now, then I will have 14 kidnapped grandchildren." However, when one of his son's ears was delivered by mail to a newspaper in Rome (delivery had been delayed by three weeks because of a postal strike), his father finally agreed to help out with the ransom payment by making the ransom payment a loan to his son. In 1976, Getty's father died. Over the next decade Getty suffered from depression and, in 1984 in a final attempt to end his drug addiction, checked himself into a London clinic. While there he received a visit from the then Prime Minister Margaret Thatcher to thank him for large donations to the National Gallery. She reportedly helped speed his recovery by telling him, "My dear Mr. Getty, we mustn't let things get us down, must we? We'll have you out of here as soon as possible." During a low period in the 1970s Getty had been cheered up by the former England cricketer and later President of the MCC, Gubby Allen, having previously been introduced to the game by Mick Jagger of the Rolling Stones.[5]

U.S. Pulls Out of Vietnam
- The peace talks then resumed, and on January 27, 1973, the parties agreed to a cease-fire the following day, the withdrawal of all U.S. forces, the release of all prisoners of war,

and the creation of an international force to keep the peace. The South Vietnamese were to have the right to determine their own future, but North Vietnamese troops stationed in the south could remain. By the end of 1973, almost all U.S. military personnel had left South Vietnam.

U.S. Vice President Resigns
- Oct. 19, less than a year before Richard M. Nixon's resignation as president of the United States, Spiro Agnew becomes the first U.S. vice president to resign in disgrace. The same day, he pleaded no contest to a charge of federal income tax evasion in exchange for the dropping of charges of political corruption. He was subsequently fined $10,000, sentenced to three years probation, and disbarred by the Maryland court of appeals.

1974

Halie Selassie, Emperor of Ethiopia, Deposed
- Coming to power in a palace coup and, later, discomfiting his enemies in battle, Haile Selassie was driven into exile by the troops of Fascist Italy after the civilized world had spurned his eloquent and poignant appeals for help.

Mikhail Baryshnikov Defects

- On June 29th, 1974, Mikhail Baryshnikov runs three blocks to a waiting car in Toronto and effectively defects from the Soviet Union. It happens shortly after the Kirov Ballet's final performance at the O'Keefe Centre. Baryshnikov was in the city as part of the company's Canadian tour. The 26-year-old's high-stakes defection has led to a flurry of media interest.

Patty Hearst Kidnapped

- Around 9 o'clock in the evening on February 4, 1974, there was a knock on the door of apartment #4 at 2603 Benvenue Street in Berkeley, California. In burst a group of men and women with their guns drawn. They grabbed a surprised 19-year-old college student named Patty Hearst, beat up her fiancé, threw her in the trunk of their car and drove off.
- Thus began one of the strangest cases in FBI history.
- Hearst, it was soon discovered, had been kidnapped by a group of armed radicals that billed themselves as the Symbionese Liberation Army, or SLA. Led by a hardened criminal named Donald DeFreeze, the SLA wanted nothing less than to incite a guerrilla war against the U.S. government and destroy what they called the "capitalist state." Their ranks included women

and men, blacks and whites, and anarchists and extremists from various walks in life.
- They were, in short, a band of domestic terrorists. And dangerous ones. They'd already shot two Oakland school officials with cyanide-tipped bullets, killing one and seriously wounding the other.
- Assault rifle in hand, Hearst joins DeFreeze in robbing a San Franciso bank on April 15, 1974. It was her first crime as a professed SLA member.
- Why'd they snatch Hearst? To get the country's attention, primarily. Hearst was from a wealthy, powerful family; her grandfather was the newspaper magnate William Randolph Hearst. The SLA's plan worked and worked well: the kidnapping stunned the country and made front-page national news.
- But the SLA had more plans for Patty Hearst. Soon after her disappearance, the SLA began releasing audiotapes demanding millions of dollars in food donations in exchange for her release. At the same time, they apparently began abusing and brainwashing their captive, hoping to turn this young heiress from the highest reaches of society into a poster child for their coming revolution.
- That, too, seemed to work. On April 3, the SLA released a tape with Hearst saying that she'd

joined their fight to free the oppressed and had even taken a new name. A dozen days later, she was spotted on bank surveillance cameras wielding an assault weapon during an SLA bank robbery, barking orders to bystanders and providing cover to her confederates.
- Assault rifle in hand, Hearst joins DeFreeze in robbing a San Franciso bank on April 15, 1974. It was her first crime as a professed SLA member.
- Meanwhile, the FBI had launched one of the most massive, agent-intensive searches in its history to find Hearst and stop the SLA. Working with many partners, we ran down thousands of leads. But with the SLA frightening potential informants into silence, using good operational security, and relying on an organized network of safe houses, it was tough going.
- A break came in Los Angeles. On May 16, two SLA members tried to steal an ammunition belt from a local store and were nearly caught. The getaway van was discovered, which led authorities to an SLA safe house. The next day, the house was surrounded by L.A. police. A massive shootout ensued. The building went up in flames; six members of the SLA died in the blaze, including DeFreeze.
- But where was Hearst? She and several others had escaped and began traveling around the

country to avoid capture. FBI agents, though, were close behind. We finally captured her in San Francisco on September 18, 1975, and she was charged with bank robbery and other crimes.
- Her trial was as sensational as the chase. Despite claims of brainwashing, the jury found her guilty, and she was sentenced to seven years in prison. Hearst served two years before President Carter commuted her sentence. She was later pardoned.
- And the rest of the SLA? We caught up with them all. The last two members were arrested in 1999 and 2002. Case closed.

Terracotta Army Discovered in China
- On March 29, 1974, three farmers were drilling holes in the hopes of finding water to dig wells when they came upon some ancient terracotta pottery shards. It didn't take long for news of this discovery to spread and by July a Chinese archaeological team began excavating the site.
- What these farmers had discovered was the 2200-year-old remains of a life-sized, terracotta army which had been buried with Qin Shihuangdi, the man who had united the varied provinces of China and thus became the very first emperor of China (221-210 BCE).

U.S. President Nixon Resigns

- Aug. 8, just before noon, Nixon officially ended his term as the 37th president of the United States. Before departing with his family in a helicopter from the White House lawn, he smiled farewell and enigmatically raised his arms in a victory or peace salute. The helicopter door was then closed, and the Nixon family began their journey home to San Clemente, California. Minutes later, Vice President Gerald R. Ford was sworn in as the 38th president of the United States in the East Room of the White House. After taking the oath of office, President Ford spoke to the nation in a television address, declaring, "My fellow Americans, our long national nightmare is over." He later pardoned Nixon for any crimes he may have committed while in office, explaining that he wanted to end the national divisions created by the Watergate scandal.

1975

Arthur Ashe First Black Man to Win Wimbledon

- On July 5, 1975, Arthur Ashe became the first black man to win Wimbledon, defeating Jimmy Connors in a shocking upset.

Cambodian Genocide Begins
- By 1975, the U.S. had withdrawn its troops from Vietnam. Cambodia's government, plagued by corruption and incompetence, also lost its American military support. Taking advantage of the opportunity, Pol Pot's Khmer Rouge army, consisting of teenage peasant guerrillas, marched into Phnom Penh and on April 17 effectively seized control of Cambodia.
- Once in power, Pol Pot began a radical experiment to create an agrarian utopia inspired in part by Mao Zedong's Cultural Revolution which he had witnessed first-hand during a visit to Communist China.

Civil War in Lebanon
- The spark that ignited the civil war in Lebanon occurred in Beirut on April 13, 1975, when gunmen killed four Phalangists during an attempt on Pierre Jumayyil's life. Perhaps believing the assassins to have been Palestinian, the Phalangists retaliated later that day by attacking a bus carrying Palestinian passengers across a Christian neighborhood, killing about twenty-six of the occupants. The next day fighting erupted in earnest, with Phalangists pitted against Palestinian militiamen (thought by some observers to be from the Popular Front for the

Liberation of Palestine). The confessional layout of Beirut's various quarters facilitated random killing. Most Beirutis stayed inside their homes during these early days of battle, and few imagined that the street fighting they were witnessing was the beginning of a war that was to devastate their city and divide the country.

Microsoft Founded
- It's the 1970s. At work, we rely on typewriters. If we need to copy a document, we likely use a mimeograph or carbon paper. Few have heard of microcomputers, but two young computer enthusiasts, Bill Gates and Paul Allen, see that personal computing is a path to the future.
- In 1975, Gates and Allen form a partnership called Microsoft. Like most start-ups, Microsoft begins small, but has a huge vision—a computer on every desktop and in every home. During the next years, Microsoft begins to change the ways we work.

1976

Nadia Comaneci Given Seven Perfect Tens
- [July 18] MONTREAL, Canada--With a total of seven perfect ten scores at Montreal 1976 Games, Olympic legend Nadia Comaneci set a

world record for the most 10 scores at a single edition of the Olympic Games. She captured the hearts of the world and became the first gymnast in history to know what it's like to be perfect- setting also the world record for the first award of a score of perfect 10 at an Olympics Games gymnastic event.

North and South Vietnam Join to Form the Socialist Republic of Vietnam

- In 1975 North Vietnam broke the peace treaty and attacked South Vietnam once again. Without the logistic and air support of the Americans the ARVN shot off what ammunition they had left then scattered. You can not fight tanks with bayonets. North Vietnam overran South Vietnam and declared the two countries The Socialist Republic of Vietnam. Communist forces also overthrew the governments in Laos and Cambodia proving the Domino Theory was correct.
- While consolidating their victory over the next five to ten years more then 5,000,000 Southeast Asians were murdered by the Communists. Millions more were imprisoned and/or forced to flee for their lives in the largest migration of refugees since the end of WW II.

Tangshan Earthquake Kills Over 240,000
- At 3:42 a.m. on July 28, 1976, a magnitude 7.8 earthquake hit the sleeping city of Tangshan, in northeastern China. The very large earthquake, striking an area where it was totally unexpected, obliterated the city of Tangshan and killed over 240,000 people - making it the deadliest earthquake of the twentieth century

1977

Elvis Found Dead
- Elvis Presley died at Graceland on August 16, 1977. He was 42 years old.
- Through the early morning of the 16th Elvis took care of last minute tour details and relaxed with family and staff. He was to fly to Portland, Maine that night and do a show there on the 17th, then continue the scheduled tour.
- Elvis retired to his master suite at Graceland around 7:00 AM to rest for his evening flight. By late morning, Elvis Presley had died of heart failure.

Miniseries Roots Airs
- Two of the most important American television programs are "The Civil War" by Ken Burns (1989), and the epic narrative miniseries "Roots" (1977) based on the book "Roots: The

Saga of an American Family" by Alex Haley. Despite the controversy surrounding the book, and the facts of Haley's ancestry (for example, the slave Toby aka "Kunte Kinte", may never have fathered Kizzy and therefore may not be a direct ancestor of Haley) the series is an important and ground-breaking work in its stunning portrayal of slave life in America from the late 18th century to the mid-19th century.

South African Anti-Apartheid Leader Steve Biko Tortured to Death

- On 12 September 1977, Stephen Bantu Biko died in a prison cell in Pretoria. The announcement of Biko's death by the South African government the next day sparked international and national protest. Steve Biko was not the only person to die in detention at the hands of the South African security police; yet, because of Biko's prominence as a charismatic leader of the Black Consciousness Movement, his case captured the attention of many South Africans and people throughout the world.

Star Wars Movie Released

- Science-fiction fans and movie buffs in general have cause to celebrate, May 25 1977, when 20th Century Fox releases George Lucas' space odyssey Star Wars.

1978

First Test-Tube Baby Born
- July 25, 1978, Louise Joy Brown, the world's first baby to be conceived via in vitro fertilization (IVF) is born at Oldham and District General Hospital in Manchester, England, to parents Lesley and Peter Brown. The healthy baby was delivered shortly before midnight by caesarean section and weighed in at five pounds, 12 ounces.

John Paul II Becomes Pope
- In 1978, John Paul made history by becoming the first non-Italian pope in more than four hundred years. As the leader of the Catholic Church, he traveled the world, visiting more than 100 countries to spread his message of faith and peace. But he was close to home when he faced the greatest threat to his life. In 1981, an assassin shot John Paul twice in St. Peter's Square in Vatican City. Fortunately, he was able to recover from his injuries and later forgave his attacker.

Jonestown Massacre
- The Jonestown Massacre, which had a death toll of 918 people, was the most deadly

single non-natural disaster in U.S. history until September 11, 2001. The Jonestown Massacre also remains the only time in history in which a U.S. congressman was killed in the line of duty.

1979

Ayatollah Khomeini Returns as Leader of Iran

- On February 1, 1979, the Ayatollah Khomeini returns to Iran in triumph after 15 years of exile. The shah and his family had fled the country two weeks before, and jubilant Iranian revolutionaries were eager to establish a fundamentalist Islamic government under Khomeini's leadership.

Iran Takes American Hostages in Tehran

- On November 4, 1979, an angry mob of some 300 to 500 "students" who called themselves "Imam's Disciples," laid siege to the American Embassy in Teheran, Iran, to capture and hold hostage 66 U.S. citizens and diplomats. Although women and African-Americans were released a short time later, 51 hostages remained imprisoned for 444 days with another individual released because of illness midway through the ordeal.

Margaret Thatcher First Woman Prime Minister of Great Britain

- Margaret Thatcher (1925-2013), the United Kingdom's first and thus far only female prime minister, served from 1979 until 1990. During her time in office, she reduced the influence of trade unions, privatized certain industries, scaled back public benefits and changed the terms of political debate, much like her friend and ideological ally, U.S. President Ronald Reagan. Nicknamed the "Iron Lady," she opposed Soviet communism and fought a war to maintain control of the Falkland Islands. The longest-serving British prime minister of the 20th century, Thatcher was eventually pressured into resigning by members of her own Conservative Party

Mother Teresa Awarded the Nobel Peace Prize

- Mother Teresa was the recipient of numerous honors including the 1979 Nobel Peace Prize. In late 2003, she was beatified, the third step toward possible sainthood, giving her the title "Blessed Teresa of Calcutta". A second miracle credited to her intercession is required before she can be recognized as a saint by the Catholic Church.

Nuclear Accident at Three Mile Island

- The Three Mile Island power station is near Harrisburg, Pennsylvania in USA. It had two pressurized water reactors. The accident to unit 2 happened at 4 am on 28 March 1979 when the reactor was operating at 97% power. It involved a relatively minor malfunction in the secondary cooling circuit which caused the temperature in the primary coolant to rise. This in turn caused the reactor to shut down automatically. Shut down took about one second. At this point a relief valve failed to close, but instrumentation did not reveal the fact, and so much of the primary coolant drained away that the residual decay heat in the reactor core was not removed. The core suffered severe damage as a result.
- The operators were unable to diagnose or respond properly to the unplanned automatic shutdown of the reactor. Deficient control room instrumentation and inadequate emergency response training proved to be root causes of the accident

Inventions & Events

Inventions & Events

Reagan '80-'88   G.H.W. Bush '88-'92

1980 1989 - Inventions

Many of the most popular consumer products still around today were invented in the 80s for example: cell phones and home computers. The 80s saw the rise of the multi-national corporations, while the growth rate during the 80s was 3.2% per year, the highest 9 year rate in American history, a complex combination of causes (economic, financial, legislative and regulatory) led to the extraordinary number of bank failures in the 80s.
And a new definition of the expression "corporate greed" was found.

1980

The hepatitis-B vaccine invented.
- Baruch Blumberg was the American research physician whose discovery of an antigen that provokes antibody response against hepatitis B led to the development by other researchers of a successful vaccine against the disease.
- Hepatitis A is a liver disease caused by the hepatitis A virus (HAV). Hepatitis A can affect anyone. In the United States, hepatitis A can occur in situations ranging from isolated cases of disease to widespread epidemics. Hepatitis B is a serious disease caused by a virus that attacks the liver. The virus, which is called hepatitis B virus (HBV), can cause lifelong infection, cirrhosis (scarring) of the liver, liver cancer, liver failure, and death. Hepatitis C is a liver disease caused by the Hepatitis C virus (HCV), which is found in the blood of persons who have the disease. HCV is spread by contact with the blood of an infected person.

1981

Inventions & Events

MS-DOS invented.
- In 1980, IBM first approached Bill Gates of Microsoft, to discuss the state of home computers and what Microsoft products could do for IBM. Gates gave IBM a few ideas on what would make a great home computer, among them to have Basic written into the ROM chip. Microsoft had already produced several versions of Basic for different computer system beginning with the Altair, so Gates was more than happy to write a version for IBM.
- As for an operating system (OS) for an IBM computer, since Microsoft had never written an operating system before, Gates had suggested that IBM investigate an OS called CP/M (Control Program for Microcomputers), written by Gary Kildall of Digital Research. Kindall had his Ph.D. in computers and had written the most successful operating system of the time, selling over 600,000 copies of CP/M, his operating system set the standard at that time.
- IBM tried to contact Gary Kildall for a meeting, executives met with Mrs Kildall who refused to sign a non-disclosure agreement. IBM soon returned to Bill Gates and gave Microsoft the contract to write a new operating system, one that would eventually wipe Gary Kildall's CP/M out of common use.

Inventions & Events

- The "Microsoft Disk Operating System" or MS-DOS was based on Microsoft's purchase of QDOS, the "Quick and Dirty Operating System" written by Tim Paterson of Seattle Computer Products, for their prototype Intel 8086 based computer.
- However, ironically QDOS was based (or copied from as some historians feel) on Gary Kildall's CP/M. Tim Paterson had bought a CP/M manual and used it as the basis to write his operating system in six weeks. QDOS was different enough from CP/M to be considered legally a different product. IBM had deep enough pockets in any case to probably have won an infringement case, if they had needed to protect their product. Microsoft bought the rights to QDOS for $50,000, keeping the IBM & Microsoft deal a secret from Tim Paterson and his company, Seattle Computer Products.
- Bill Gates then talked IBM into letting Microsoft retain the rights, to market MS-DOS separate from the IBM PC project, Gates and Microsoft proceeded to make a fortune from the licensing of MS-DOS. In 1981, Tim Paterson quit Seattle Computer Products and found employment at Microsoft.
- "Life begins with a disk drive." - Tim Paterson

Inventions & Events

The first IBM-PC invented.
- IBM's own Personal Computer (IBM 5150) was introduced in August 1981, only a year after corporate executives gave the go-ahead to Bill Lowe, the lab director in the company's Boca Raton, Fla., facilities. He set up a task force that developed the proposal for the first IBM PC. Early studies had concluded that there were not enough applications to justify acceptance on a broad basis and the task force was fighting the idea that things couldn't be done quickly in IBM. One analyst was quoted as saying that "IBM bringing out a personal computer would be like teaching an elephant to tap dance." During a meeting with top executives in New York, Lowe claimed his group could develop a small, new computer within a year. The response: "You're on. Come back in two weeks with a proposal."
- Lowe picked a group of 12 strategists who worked around the clock to hammer out a plan for hardware, software, manufacturing setup and sales strategy. It was so well-conceived that the basic strategy remained unaltered throughout the product cycle.

The scanning tunneling microscope invented by Gerd Karl Binnig and Heinrich Rohrer.
- The scanning tunneling microscope (STM) is widely used in both industrial and fundamen-

tal research to obtain atomic-scale images of metal surfaces. It provides a three-dimensional profile of the surface which is very useful for characterizing surface roughness, observing surface defects, and determining the size and conformation of molecules and aggregates on the surface.

1982

Human growth hormone genetically engineered.
- Genetic engineering (GE) is a term for the process of manipulating genes-moving genes from one organism to another. It usually takes place outside of an organism's normal reproductive process.
- Engineering, of course, is just a fancy word for "making something"-so genetic engineering is just a fancy term for "making something with genes."
- Genetic engineering is done to introduce new characteristics into an organism-characteristics like increased crop yield or resistance to disease. The mechanism for this is usually the production of a new enzyme or protein.
- One of the most successful examples of GE is the production of human insulin through the use of modified bacteria. This was first approved in

1982 and has been saving the lives of diabetics ever since. Another is genetically engineered tissue plasminogen activator, which is expected to help prevent strokes.

1983

The Apple Lisa invented.
- Officially, "Lisa" stood for "Local Integrated Software Architecture", but it was also the name of Apple co-founder Steve Jobs' daughter.
- The Lisa is the first commercial computer with a GUI, or Graphical User Interface. Prior to the Lisa, all computers were text based - you typed commands on the keyboard to make the system respond. Now, with the Lisa, you just point-and-click at tiny pictures on the screen with a small rolling device called a 'mouse'.

Soft bifocal contact lens invented.
- Bifocal daily wear soft contact lenses became available for commercial distribution.

First Cabbage Patch Kids sold.
- In 1983, a Cabbage Patch Kids doll was a 16-inch doll, usually with a plastic head, a fabric body, and yarn hair (unless it was bald). What made them so desirable, besides the fact that

they were huggable, was both their supposed uniqueness and their adoptability.
- It was claimed that each Cabbage Patch Kids doll was unique. Different head molds, eye shapes and colors, hair styles and colors, and clothing options did make each one look different than the other. This plus the fact that inside each Cabbage Patch Kids box came a "birth certificate," with that particular kid's first and middle name on it, made the dolls as individual as the kids who wanted to adopt them.
- The official Cabbage Patch Kids story tells of a young boy named Xavier Roberts, who was led by a Bunnybee through a waterfall, down a long tunnel, and out into a magical land where a cabbage patch grew little children. When he was asked to help, Roberts agreed to find loving homes for these Cabbage Patch Kids.
- The real Xavier Roberts, who invented the Cabbage Patch Kids dolls, had no trouble "adopting" out his dolls in 1983, for real kids around the country vied to be one of the few whose parents were able to buy them one.

Programmer Jaron Lanier first coins the term "virtual reality".
- Jaron Lanier, born May 3, 1960 is an American writer, computer scientist, and composer of classical music. A pioneer in the field of

virtual reality (a term he is credited with popularizing), Lanier and Thomas G. Zimmerman left Atari in 1985 to found VPL Research, Inc., the first company to sell VR goggles and gloves.

1984

The CD-ROM invented.
- Originally the CD-ROM was invented as a way to store music in a digital format that is much more stable than magnetic tapes (8-tracks & cassettes) and smaller than an LP (record). With improvements in technology it has since been adapted to be the most convenient way to produce software for the public (1 single layer DVD ROM replaces 3,263 Floppies)

The Apple Macintosh invented.
- Apple introduced the Macintosh computer January of 1984. It was introduced during a Super Bowl commercial. They were one of the first to make a commercial look like a huge budget movie.

1985

Windows program invented by Microsoft.
- Microsoft introduced an operating environment named Windows on November 20,

1985 as a graphical operating system shell for MS-DOS in response to the growing interest in graphical user interfaces (GUIs). Microsoft Windows came to dominate the world's personal computer market with over 90% market share, overtaking Mac OS, which had been introduced in 1984.

1986

A high-temperature super-conductor invented by J. Georg Bednorz and Karl A. Muller.
- In 1986, Georg Bednorz and Alex Mueller, working at IBM in Zurich Switzerland, were experimenting with a particular class of metal oxide ceramics called perovskites. Georg Bednorz and Alex Mueller surveyed hundreds of different oxide compounds. Working with ceramics of lanthanum, barium, copper, and oxygen they found indications of superconductivity at 35 K, a startling 12 K above the old record for a superconductor. Soon researchers from around the world would be working with the new types of superconductors.

Synthetic skin invented by G. Gregory Gallico, III.
- Synthetic Skin invented by G. Gregory Gallico, III. 1986

- Allowed those with prosthetic limbs to feel the sense of touch.
- Used to replace skin lost in traumatic events or due to disease.

Fuji introduced the disposable camera.
- The Fujicolor QuickSnap was marketed in 1986 as the world's first single-use camera and immediately recorded enormous sales. It soon became known for its simple functionality and a very low part count.

1987

The first 3-D video game invented.
- Most people would say that the first 3-D game was Battlezone, which was originally released in 1980. Battlezone used a 3-D wireframe environment.

Disposable contact lenses invented.
- Disposable contacts are worn for a specific period of time, then thrown out and replaced with fresh lenses. Disposables have become the most common type of contact lenses.

1988

Inventions & Events

Digital cellular phones invented.
- One of the most important years in cell phone evolution. The Cellular Technology Industry Association is created and helps to make the industry into an empire. One of its biggest contributions is when it helped create TDMA phone technology, the most evolved cell phone yet. It becomes available to the public in 1991.

The RU-486 (abortion pill) invented.
- In September, 1988, the French government approved the distribution of RU-486 for use in government-controlled clinics. The next month, however, Roussel Uclaf stopped selling the drug because people opposed to abortion did not want RU-486 to be available and were threatening to boycott the company. Then, however, there were threats and pressure from the other side. For example, members of the World Congress of Obstetrics and Gynecology announced that they might boycott Roussel Uclaf if it did not make RU-486 available. The French government, which controlled a 36 percent interest in Roussel Uclaf, ordered the company to start distributing the drug once more. By the fall of 1989, more than one-fourth of all early abortions in France were being done with RU-486 and a prostaglandin. The French government began helping to pay the cost of using RU-486

in 1990. Testing for approval of RU-486 was completed in Great Britain and The Netherlands, but Roussel Uclaf's parent company, Hoechst AG, did not try to market the drug there or in any other country outside France. (In the United States, government regulations did not allow RU-486 to be tested using government funds.) Medical researchers believe that RU-486 may be useful not only for abortions but also in other ways. For example, it may help in treating certain breast cancers and other tumors. RU-486 is also being investigated as a possible treatment for glaucoma-to lower pressure in the eye that may be caused by a high level of steroid hormone. It may be useful in promoting the healing of skin wounds and softening the cervix at birth, easing delivery. Researchers hope as well that some form of RU-486 may prove useful as a contraceptive-that is, not to prevent a fertilized egg from implanting itself in the mother's uterus but to prevent ovulation in the first place.

Doppler radar invented by Christian Andreas Doppler.
- Doppler RADAR is named after Christian Andreas Doppler. Doppler was an Austrian physicist who first described in 1842, how the observed frequency of light and sound waves

was affected by the relative motion of the source and the detector. This phenomenon became known as the Doppler effect.
- This is most often demonstrated by the change in the sound wave of a passing train. The sound of the train whistle will become "higher" in pitch as it approaches and "lower" in pitch as it moves away. This is explained as follows: the number of sound waves reaching the ear in a given amount of time (this is called the frequency) determines the tone, or pitch, perceived. The tone remains the same as long as you are not moving. As the train moves closer to you the number of sound waves reaching your ear in a given amount of time increases. Thus, the pitch increases. As the train moves away from you the opposite happens.

Prozac invented at the Eli Lilly Company by inventor Ray Fuller.
-     Prozac is the registered trademarked name for fluoxetine hydrochloride and the world's most widely prescribed antidepressant to-date, the first product in a major new class of drugs for depression called selective serotonin re-uptake inhibitors. Prozac was first introduced to the US market in January 1988. It took two years for Prozac to gain its 'most prescribed' status.

The first patent for a genetically engineered animal is issued to Harvard University researchers Philip Leder and Timothy Stewart.
- Calling it a ``singularly historic event,`` the United States on Tuesday issued to Harvard University the world`s first patent for a higher form of life, a genetically engineered mouse created by researchers at Harvard Medical School.
- The U.S. Patent and Trademark Office issued patent No. 4,736,866 for ``transgenic non-human mammals`` developed by Dr. Philip Leder, 53, a geneticist at Harvard Medical College in Boston, and Dr. Timothy A. Stewart, 35, a former Harvard researcher who is a senior scientist at Genentech Inc., a leading biotechnology company in south San Francisco.

1989

High-definition television invented.
- Modern-day HDTV has its roots in research that was started in Japan by the NHK (Japan Broadcasting Corporation) in 1970. In 1977, the SMPTE (The Society of Motion Picture and Television Engineers) Study Group on High Definition Television was formed. The group published its initial recommendations in 1980, which

included, among other things, the definition of wide screen format and 1100-line scanning structure. The first demonstration of HDTV in the United States took place in 1981 and generated a great deal of interest. In 1987, the FCC (Federal Communications Commission) sought advice from the private sector and formed the Advisory Committee on Advanced Television Service. Initially, there were as many as 23 different ATV (Advanced Television) systems proposed to this committee, but by 1990, there were only 9 proposals remaining - all based on analog technology. However, by mid-1991, the leading ATV designs were based on a new all-digital approach. A joint proposal from several companies detailing an all-digital ATV system was given to the FCC in 1995. Following certain changes and compromises, this proposal was approved by the FCC in December, 1996 and became the mandated ATSC (Advanced Television Systems Committee) standard for terrestrial DTV/HDTV broadcasting.

1980 - 1989 - Events

1980

Failed U.S. Rescue Attempt to Save Hostages in Tehran
- On April 24, 1980, an ill-fated military operation to rescue the 52 American hostages held in Tehran ends with eight U.S. servicemen dead and no hostages rescued.
- With the Iran Hostage Crisis stretching into its sixth month and all diplomatic appeals to the Iranian government ending in failure, President Jimmy Carter ordered the military mission as a last ditch attempt to save the hostages. During the operation, three of eight helicopters failed, crippling the crucial airborne plans. The mission was then canceled at the staging area in Iran, but during the withdrawal one of the retreating helicopters collided with one of six C-130 transport planes, killing eight soldiers and injuring five. The next day, a somber Jimmy Carter gave a press conference in which he took full responsibility for the tragedy. The hostages were not released for another 270 days.

John Lennon Assassinated
- The Beatles' musician John Lennon was shot and killed outside of his New York City

apartment on the night of Dec. 8, 1980. Lennon and wife Yoko Ono were returning from the recording studio to their home at The Dakota when 25-year-old crazed fan Mark David Chapman shot him at close range. Earlier in the day Chapman had been hanging around The Dakota with other fans and asked Lennon for an autograph.
- When The Beatles broke up in 1970, John Lennon focused on humanitarian and social activism. After the 1975 birth of his son Sean, John Lennon retreated from public eye to concentrate on his family. John Lennon and Yoko Ono's 1980 "Double-Fantasy" album was planned to be his comeback in the music scene. Lennon was murdered just weeks after "Double-Fantasy" was released.

Mount St. Helens Erupts

- Mount St. Helens erupted on May 18, 1980. The volcano, located in southwestern Washington, used to be a beautiful symmetrical cone about 9,600 feet (3,000 meters) above sea level. The eruption, which removed the upper 1,300 feet (396 meters) of the summit, left a horseshoe-shaped crater and a barren wasteland. Today the land is healing, having recovered its natural beauty, but the landscape has been permanently altered.

Inventions & Events

Pac-Man Video Game Released
- On May 22, 1980, the Pac-Man video game was released in Japan and by October of the same year it was released in the United States. The yellow, pie-shaped Pac-Man character, who travels around a maze trying to eat dots and avoid four mean ghosts, quickly became an icon of the 1980s. To this day, Pac-Man remains one of the most popular video games in history.

Rubik's Cube Becomes Popular
- It seemed like such a simple puzzle and yet the Rubik's Cube mesmerized millions of people with its complexity. The Rubik's Cube became one of the most popular toys of the twentieth century and an icon of the 1980s.
- First created in 1974; Released to world market in 1980

Ted Turner Establishes CNN
- Turner made his initial fortune by transforming a small billboard company into cable television's first "superstation," Turner Broadcasting System, in 1979. It would grow into one of the most popular basic cable options in households across America. In 1980 Turner founded CNN (Cable News Network), the first

24-hour television news channel. He also owns Turner Network Television, Turner Classic Movies, the Cartoon Network, New Line Cinema, and Castle Rock Entertainment.

1981

Assassination Attempt on the Pope

- The first attempted assassination of Pope John Paul II took place on Wednesday, 13 May 1981, in St. Peter's Square at Vatican City. The Pope was shot and wounded by Mehmet Ali Ağca while he was entering the square. The Pope was struck four times, and suffered severe blood loss. Ağca was apprehended immediately, and later sentenced to life in prison by an Italian court. The Pope later forgave Ağca for the assassination attempt.[1] He was pardoned by Italian president Carlo Azeglio Ciampi at the Pope's request and was deported to Turkey in June 2000.

Assassination Attempt on U.S. President Reagan

- The attempted assassination of Ronald Reagan occurred on Monday, March 30, 1981, 69 days into his presidency. While leaving a speaking engagement at the Washington Hilton Hotel in Washington, D.C., President Reagan

Inventions & Events

and three others were shot and wounded by John Hinckley, Jr.
- Reagan suffered a punctured lung and heavy internal bleeding, but prompt medical attention allowed him to recover quickly. Ronald Reagan was shot in the chest and in the lower right arm. No formal invocation of presidential succession took place, although Secretary of State Alexander Haig controversially stated that he was "in control here" while Vice President George H. W. Bush returned to Washington.
- Nobody was killed in the attack, though Press Secretary James Brady was left paralyzed and permanently disabled. Hinckley was found not guilty by reason of insanity and remains confined to a psychiatric facility.

First Woman Appointed to the U.S. Supreme Court

- On July 7, 1981, President Ronald Reagan nominated Sandra Day O'Connor to be the first woman on the U.S. Supreme Court. On September 21, the United States Senate confirmed O'Connor in a vote of 99 for and zero against. Sandra Day O'Connor was officially sworn in and took her seat on the U.S. Supreme Court on September 25, 1981.
- O'Connor served on the U.S. Supreme Court for over two decades. On July 1, 2005, O'Connor

announced that she would retire as soon as a successor was chosen. On January 31, 2006, Samuel Alito was sworn in, filling O'Connor's seat on the U.S. Supreme Court.

Millions Watch Royal Wedding on T.V.
- On July 20, crowds of 600,000 people filled the streets of London to catch a glimpse of Prince Charles and Lady Diana Spencer on their wedding day.
- The couple were married at St Paul's Cathedral before an invited congregation of 3,500 and an estimated global TV audience of 750 million - making it the most popular program ever broadcast.

New Plague Identified as AIDS
- In 1980 and 1981, doctors in the United States discovered that young gay men and IV-drug users, were mysteriously getting diseases most often seen when the immune system is damaged. As the months progressed, more and more people in these groups began to die from diseases associated with a damaged immune system. This trend was also beginning to be seen in Western Europe. As the numbers began to dramatically increase, it became clear that a new disease was upon us. AIDS was identified as a new disease in 1981. Human immunodefi-

ciency virus (HIV) was co-discovered several years later by Luc Montagnier and Robert Gallo.

Personal Computers (PC) Introduced by IBM

- The IBM Personal Computer, commonly known as the IBM PC, is the original version and progenitor of the IBM PC compatible hardware platform. It is IBM model number 5150, and was introduced on August 12, 1981. It was created by a team of engineers and designers under the direction of Don Estridge of the IBM Entry Systems Division in Boca Raton, Florida.

1982

E.T. Movie Released

- E.T. the Extra-Terrestrial (often referred to simply as E.T.) is a 1982 American science fiction film coproduced and directed by Steven Spielberg and written by Melissa Mathison, featuring special effects by Carlo Rambaldi and starring Henry Thomas, Dee Wallace, Robert MacNaughton, Drew Barrymore, and Peter Coyote. It tells the story of Elliott (played by Thomas), a lonely boy who befriends an extraterrestrial, dubbed "E.T.", who is stranded on Earth. Elliott and his siblings help it return home while attempting to keep it hidden from their mother and the government.

Falkland Islands Invaded by Argentina

- The Falklands War (Spanish: Guerra de las Malvinas), also known as the Falklands Conflict, Falklands Crisis and the Guerra del Atlántico Sur (Spanish for "South Atlantic War"), was a ten-week war between Argentina and the United Kingdom over two British overseas territories in the South Atlantic: the Falkland Islands and South Georgia and the South Sandwich Islands. It began on Friday 2 April 1982 when Argentina invaded and occupied the Falkland Islands (and, the following day, South Georgia and the South Sandwich Islands) in an attempt to establish the sovereignty it has long claimed over them. On 5 April, the British government dispatched a naval task force to engage the Argentine Navy and Air Force before making an amphibious assault on the islands. The conflict lasted 74 days and ended with the Argentine surrender on 14 June 1982, returning the islands to British control. 649 Argentine military personnel, 255 British military personnel and 3 Falkland Islanders died during the hostilities.King Henry VIII's Ship the Mary Rose Raised After 437 Years

Michael Jackson Releases Thriller

- Michael Jackson's legendary Thriller album was released on Nov. 30, 1982. Thriller includes Jackson's hit singles "Thriller," "Billie Jean," "The Girl Is Mine," and "Beat It." The epic zombie dance music video for "Thriller" did not debut until the following year on Dec. 2, 1983. Thriller is the best-selling album of all time, with over 100 million copies sold worldwide since the 1982 release.

Reverend Sun Myung Moon Marries 2,075 Couples at Madison Square Garden

- In a ceremony involving 2,075 couples at Madison Square Garden in 1982, for example, the men wore identical blue suits and the women lace and satin gowns. Mr. Moon was said to have made the matches, based on questionnaires, photographs and the recommendations of church officials.

Vietnam War Memorial Opened in Washington, DC

- On Nov. 10, 1982, the first visitors toured the newly completed Vietnam Veterans Memorial near the National Mall in Washington. Commonly called "The Wall," the memorial features a long V-shaped expanse bearing the names of all United States service members killed during the conflict in Vietnam/Southeast Asia.

1983

Cabbage Patch Kids Are Popular
- The Cabbage Patch Kids brand of products originally started as dolls called Little People, created by Xavier Roberts with the help of four women, and inspired by Tennessee artisan Martha Nelson.[4][5]
- The name change to Cabbage Patch Kids was instigated by Roger Smith before he secured the worldwide licensing rights to "Little People", and was the basis of the story co-authored in 1982 by Roger and his wife, Susanne Nance Schlaifer.[6] An abbreviated version of the story was reproduced on every Cabbage Patch Kids product from 1983 onward. Parker Brothers published the original story retitled "Xavier's Fantastic Discovery" in 1984 and their Parker Records produced a Gold Album using the characters. The characters appeared in many other Cabbage Patch merchandising products ranging from animated cartoons to board games.

Inventions & Events

Reagan Announces Defense Plan Called Star Wars

- On March 23, 1983, in a nationally televised address on national security, President Ronald Reagan proposed the development of the technology to intercept enemy nuclear missiles. The plan, called the Strategic Defense Initiative, or S.D.I., was dubbed "Star Wars" by its critics.

Sally Ride Becomes the First American Woman in Space

- On June 18, 1983, Sally Ride became the first American woman to fly in space when the space shuttle Challenger launched on mission STS-7.
- As one of the three mission specialists on the STS-7 mission, she played a vital role in helping the crew deploy communications satellites, conduct experiments and make use of the first Shuttle Pallet Satellite. In this image, Dr. Ride sits in the aft flight deck mission specialist's seat during deorbit preparations.

Soviets Shoot Down a Korean Airliner

- On September 1, 1983, Korean Airlines (KAL) flight 007 was on the last leg of a flight from New York City to Seoul, with a stopover in Anchorage, Alaska. As it approached its final destination, the plane began to veer far off its normal course. In just a short time, the plane flew into Russian airspace and crossed over the Kamchatka Peninsula, where some top-secret Soviet military installations were known to be located. The Soviets sent two fighters to intercept the plane. According to tapes of the conversations between the fighter pilots and Soviet ground control, the fighters quickly located the KAL flight and tried to make contact with the passenger jet. Failing to receive a response, one of the fighters fired a heat-seeking missile. KAL 007 was hit and plummeted into the Sea of Japan. All 269 people on board were killed.

U.S. Embassy in Beirut Bombed
- On this day, a suicide bomber drives a truck filled with 2,000 pounds of explosives into a U.S. Marine Corps barracks at the Beirut International Airport. The explosion killed 220 Marines, 18 sailors and three soldiers. A few minutes after that bomb went off, a second bomber drove into the basement of the nearby French paratroopers' barracks, killing 58 more people.

1984

Huge Poison Gas Leak in Bhopal, India

- During the night of December 2-3, 1984, a storage tank containing methyl isocyanate (MIC) at the Union Carbide pesticide plant leaked gas into the densely populated city of Bhopal, India. It was one of the worst industrial accidents in history.
- Union Carbide India, Ltd. built a pesticide plant in Bhopal, India in the late 1970s in an effort to produce pesticides locally to help increase production on local farms. However, sales of pesticide didn't materialize in the numbers hoped for and the plant was soon losing money. In 1979, the factory began to produce large amounts of the highly toxic methyl isocyanate (MIC), because it was a cheaper way to make the pesticide carbaryl. To also cut costs, training and maintenance in the factory were drastically cut back. Workers in the factory complained about the dangerous conditions and warned of possible disasters, but management did not take any action.
- On the night of December 2-3, 1984, something began to go wrong in storage tank E610 which contained 40 tons of MIC. Water leaked into the tank which caused the MIC to heat up. Some sources say that water leaked into the tank during routine cleaning of a pipe but that the safety valves inside the pipe were faulty. The Union

Carbide company claims that a saboteur placed the water inside the tank, although there has never been proof of this. It is also considered possible that once the tank began to overheat, workers threw water on the tank, not realizing they were adding to the problem.
- By 12:15 a.m. on the morning of December 3, 1984, MIC fumes were leaking out of the storage tank. Although there should have been six safety features that would have either prevented the leak or contained it, all six did not work properly that night. It is estimated that 27 tons of MIC gas escaped out of the container and spread across the densely populated city of Bhopal, India, which had a population of approximately 900,000 people. Although a warning siren was turned on, it was quickly turned off again so as to not cause panic.
- Most residents of Bhopal were sleeping when the gas began to leak. Many woke up only because they heard their children coughing or found themselves choking on the fumes. As people jumped up from their beds, they felt their eyes and throat burning. Some choked on their own bile. Others fell to the ground in contortions of pain.
- People ran and ran, but they did not know in which direction to go. Families were split up in

the confusion. Many people fell to the ground unconscious and were then trampled upon.
- Estimates of the death toll vary greatly. Most sources say at least 3,000 people died from immediate exposure to the gas, while higher estimates go up to 8,000. In the two decades following the night of the disaster, approximately 20,000 additional people have died from the damage they received from the gas.
- Another 120,000 people live daily with the effects from the gas, including blindness, extreme shortness of breath, cancers, birth deformities, and early onset of menopause. Chemicals from the pesticide plant and from the leak have infiltrated the water system and the soil near the old factory and thus continue to cause poisoning in the people who live near it.

Indira Gandhi, India's Prime Minister, Killed by Two Bodyguards

- As she passed a wicket gate guarded by Satwant Singh and Beant Singh, they opened fire. Sub-Inspector Beant Singh fired three rounds into her abdomen from his sidearm.[5] Satwant Singh then fired 30 rounds from his Sten gun into her after she had fallen to the ground.[5] After the shooting, both threw their weapons down and Beant Singh said "I have done what I had to do. You do what you want to do." In the next six minutes Tarsem Singh Jamwal and Ram Saran, soldiers in the Indo-Tibetan Border Police, captured and killed Beant Singh in a separate room because Beant Singh allegedly tried to pull a gun on the officers in the room.[6] Satwant Singh was arrested by Gandhi's other bodyguards along with an accomplice trying to escape, and was seriously wounded in the attack initiated by Beant Singh.[7] Satwant Singh was hanged in 1989 with accomplice Kehar Singh.

PG-13 Movie Rating Created
- July 1, 1984, the Motion Picture Association of America (MPAA), which oversees the voluntary rating system for movies, introduces a new rating, PG-13.

1985

Famine in Ethiopia
- The great famine of 1983–5 is often ascribed to drought, and while climatic causes and consequences certainly played a part in the tragedy, it has been shown that widespread drought occurred only some months after the famine was under way. The famines that struck Ethiopia between 1961 and 1985, and in particular the one of 1983–5, were in large part creat-

ed by government policies, specifically the set of counter-insurgency strategies employed and so-called 'social transformation' in non-insurgent areas.

Hole in the Ozone Layer Discovered
- In 1985, scientists startled the world with an ominous discovery. While monitoring the stratosphere over Antarctica, they discovered a hole in the earth's ozone layer.

Mikhail Gorbachev Calls for Glasnost and Perestroika
- When Mikhail S. Gorbachev (1931-) became general secretary of the Communist Party of the Soviet Union in March 1985, he launched his nation on a dramatic new course. His dual program of "perestroika" ("restructuring") and "glasnost" ("openness") introduced profound changes in economic practice, internal affairs and international relations. Within five years, Gorbachev's revolutionary program swept communist governments throughout Eastern Europe from power and brought an end to the Cold War (1945-91), the largely political and economic rivalry between the Soviets and the United States and their respective allies that emerged following World War II. Gorbachev's actions also inadvertently set the stage for the

1991 collapse of the Soviet Union, which dissolved into 15 individual republics. He resigned from office on December 25, 1991.

New Coke Hits the Market
- To hear some tell it, April 23, 1985, was a day that will live in marketing infamy.
- On that day, The Coca-Cola Company took arguably the biggest risk in consumer goods history, announcing that it was changing the formula for the world's most popular soft drink, and spawning consumer angst the likes of which no business has ever seen.

Wreck of the Titanic Found
- American Robert D. Ballard headed the expedition, which used an experimental, unmanned submersible developed by the U.S. Navy to search for the ocean liner. The Argo traveled just above the ocean floor, sending photographs up to the research vessel Knorr. In the early morning of September 1, Argo was investigating debris on the ocean floor when it suddenly passed over one of the Titanic's massive boilers, lying at a depth of about 13,000 feet. The wreck was subsequently explored by manned and unmanned submersibles, which shed new light on the details of its 1912 sinking.

1986

Space Shuttle Challenger Explodes
- On January 28, 1986, the American shuttle orbiter Challenger broke up 73 seconds after liftoff, bringing a devastating end to the spacecraft's 10th mission. The disaster claimed the lives of all seven astronauts aboard, including Christa McAuliffe, a teacher from New Hampshire who had been selected to join the mission and teach lessons from space to schoolchildren around the country. It was later determined that two rubber O-rings, which had been designed to separate the sections of the rocket booster, had failed due to cold temperatures on the morning of the launch. The tragedy and its aftermath received extensive media coverage and prompted NASA to temporarily suspend all shuttle missions.

Chernobyl Nuclear Disaster
- At 1:23 a.m. on April 26th, 1986, reactor four at the nuclear power plant near Chernobyl, Ukraine exploded, releasing more than a hundred times the radiation of the bombs dropped on Hiroshima and Nagasaki. Thirty-one people died shortly after the explosion and thousands more are expected to die from the long-term effects of radiation. The Chernobyl nuclear disas-

ter dramatically changed the world's opinion about using nuclear reaction for power.

Ferdinand Marcos Flees the Philippines

- In the face of mass demonstrations against his rule, Philippines President Ferdinand Marcos and his entourage are airlifted from the presidential palace in Manila by U.S. helicopters.
- Elected in 1966, Marcos declared martial law in 1972 in response to leftist violence. In the next year, he assumed dictatorial powers. Backed by the United States, his regime was marked by misuse of foreign support, repression, and political murders. In 1986, Marcos defrauded the electorate in a presidential election, declaring himself the victor over Corazon Aquino, the wife of an assassinated rival. Aquino also declared herself the rightful winner, and the public rallied behind her. Deserted by his former supporters, Marcos and his wife, Imelda, fled to Hawaii in exile, where they faced investigation on embezzlement charges. He died in 1989.

Iran-Contra Scandal Unfolds

- The Iran-Contra Affair was a clandestine action not approved of by the United States Congress. It began in 1985, when President Ronald Reagan's administration supplied weapons to Iran[1] — a sworn enemy — in hopes of securing the release of American hostages held in Lebanon by Hezbollah terrorists loyal to the Ayatollah Khomeini, Iran's leader. This article is rooted in the Iran Hostage Crisis.

- The U.S. took millions of dollars from the weapons sale and routed them and guns to the right-wing "Contra"[2] guerrillas in Nicaragua. The Contras were the armed opponents of Nicaragua's Sandinista Junta of National Reconstruction, following the July 1979 overthrow of strongman Anastasio Somoza Debayle and the ending of the Somoza family's 43-year reign.

U.S. Bombs Libya

- On April 14, 1986, the United States launches air strikes against Libya in retaliation for the Libyan sponsorship of terrorism against American troops and citizens. The raid, which began shortly before 7 p.m. EST (2 a.m., April 15 in Libya), involved more than 100 U.S. Air Force and Navy aircraft, and was over within an hour. Five military targets and "terrorism centers" were hit, including the headquarters of Libyan leader Muammar al-Qaddafi.

U.S.S.R. Launches Mir Space Station
- Mir was the first permanent space station. The station was in orbit for 13 years, and staffed continuously for the last 9 years. The complex weighed more than 100 tons and consists of the Mir core, Kvant, Kvant 2, Kristall, Spektr, Priroda and Docking modules. Mir measured more than 107 feet long with docked Progress-M and Soyuz-TM spacecraft, and is about 90 feet wide across its modules.

1987

DNA First Used to Convict Criminals
- With the exception of identical twins all humans have a unique set of DNA that is presented in their hair, skin, blood and other body fluids. Because of this genetic fingerprint, forensic testing has become an invaluable source of physical evidence for law enforcement in obtaining convictions and in exonerating the wrongly accused. In 1985, Professor Alec Jeffreys of the University of Leicester discovered that each person carried a genetic fingerprint in his or her DNA. This discovery was first put to the test in an immigration case; a year later, DNA profiling was used in a criminal case---a double homicide in England---and helped prove the innocence of a man who gave police a false confession. The

DNA obtained from crime scenes in 1983 and 1986 proved that the same man raped and killed the two young girls. With the killer's DNA on file and new crime fighting technology at their disposal, police collected blood samples from more than 5,000 men in the community. The killer was eventually caught.
- In the United States, in 1987, a rapist in Florida was the first person to be convicted through the use of DNA evidence.

Klaus Barbie, the Nazi Butcher of Lyons, Sentenced to Life in Prison

- On the 3 July 1987 Klaus Barbie was sentenced to life imprisonment for crimes against humanity. Nine jurors and three judges found Barbie – known as the "Butcher of Lyons" – guilty of the 341 separate charges that were brought against him at the court in Lyon.
- The 73-year old former Gestapo chief was accused of deporting 842 people – mainly Jews – to concentration camps during the Second World War.
- Klaus Barbie died of cancer in prison on the 25 September 1991.

New York Stock Exchange Suffers Huge Drop on "Black Monday"
- The New York Stock Exchange on Black Monday, 19 October 1987. The Dow Jones dropped over 500 points, the largest decline in modern time, as panic selling swept Wall Street.

West German Pilot Lands Unchallenged in Russia's Red Square
- On May 28, 1987, a nineteen-year-old pilot enthusiast from Germany Matthias Rust crossed Soviet territory unlawfully and unchallenged and landed his small "Cessna-172" airplane in the heart of the USSR – Red Square in Moscow.

1988

Pan Am Flight 103 Is Bombed Over Lockerbie
- By 6:56 p.m., the plane had reached 31,000 feet. At 7:03 p.m., the plane exploded. Control had just been issuing Flight 103's clearance to start its oceanic segment of their journey to New York, when Flight 103's blip went off their radar. Seconds later the one large blip was replaced with multiple blips traveling downwind.
- For the residents of Lockerbie, Scotland, their nightmare was just about to begin. "It was like meteors falling from the sky," described resident Ann McPhail (Newsweek, Jan. 2, 1989, pg. 17).

Flight 103 was over Lockerbie when it exploded. Many residents described the sky lighting up and a large, deafening roar.
- They soon saw pieces of the plane as well as pieces of bodies landing in fields, in backyards, on fences, and on rooftops. Fuel from the plane was already on fire before it hit the ground; some of it landed on houses, making the houses explode.
- One of the plane's wings hit the ground in the southern area of Lockerbie. It hit the ground with such impact that it created a crater 155 feet long, displacing approximately 1500 tons of dirt. The nose of the airplane landed mostly intact in a field about four miles from the town of Lockerbie. Many said the nose reminded them of a fish's head cut off from its body.
- Wreckage was strewn over 50 square miles. Twenty-one of Lockerbie's houses were completely destroyed and eleven of its residents were dead. Thus, the total death toll was 270 (the 259 aboard the plane plus the 11 on the ground).

U.S. Shoots Down Iranian Airliner
- Iran Air Flight 655 was an Iran Air civilian passenger flight from Tehran to Dubai that was shot down by the United States Navy guided missile cruiser USS Vincennes on 3 July 1988.

The attack took place in Iranian airspace, over Iran's territorial waters in the Persian Gulf, and on the flight's usual flight path. The aircraft, an Airbus A300 B2-203, was destroyed by SM-2MR surface-to-air missiles fired from the Vincennes.

1989

Berlin Wall Falls

- On August 13, 1961, the Communist government of the German Democratic Republic (GDR, or East Germany) began to build a barbed wire and concrete "Antifascistischer Schutzwall," or "antifascist bulwark," between East and West Berlin. The official purpose of this Berlin Wall was to keep Western "fascists" from entering East Germany and undermining the socialist state, but it primarily served the objective of stemming mass defections from East to West. The Berlin Wall stood until November 9, 1989, when the head of the East German Communist Party announced that citizens of the GDR could cross the border whenever they pleased. That night, ecstatic crowds swarmed the wall. Some crossed freely into West Berlin, while others brought hammers and picks and began to chip away at the wall itself. To this day, the Berlin Wall remains one of the most powerful and enduring symbols of the Cold War.

Exxon Valdez Spills Millions of Gallons of Oil on Coastline
- The Exxon Valdez oil spill occurred in Prince William Sound, Alaska, on March 24, 1989, when Exxon Valdez, an oil tanker bound for Long Beach, California, struck Prince William Sound's Bligh Reef at 12:04 a.m. local time and spilled 260,000 to 750,000 barrels (41,000 to 119,000 m3) of crude oil over the next few days.

Romanian Leader Nicolae Ceausescu and His Wife Are Executed
- Nicolae Ceausescu, who was executed with his wife on Christmas day of 1989, was a maverick and despotic Rumanian Communist leader who pursued an independent course abroad and demanded slavish subservience at home.

Students Massacred in China's Tiananmen Square
- In May 1989, nearly a million Chinese, mostly young students, crowded into central Beijing to protest for greater democracy and call for the resignations of Chinese Communist Party leaders deemed too repressive. For nearly

three weeks, the protesters kept up daily vigils, and marched and chanted. Western reporters captured much of the drama for television and newspaper audiences in the United States and Europe. On June 4, 1989, however, Chinese troops and security police stormed through Tiananmen Square, firing indiscriminately into the crowds of protesters. Turmoil ensued, as tens of thousands of the young students tried to escape the rampaging Chinese forces. Other protesters fought back, stoning the attacking troops and overturning and setting fire to military vehicles. Reporters and Western diplomats on the scene estimated that at least 300, and perhaps thousands, of the protesters had been killed and as many as 10,000 were arrested.

Inventions & Events

G.H.W. Bush '88-'92   Clinton '92-2000

1990 - 1999 - Inventions

1990

The World Wide Web and Internet protocol (HTTP) and WWW language (HTML) created by Tim Berners-Lee.
- Tim Berners-Lee was the man leading the development of the World Wide Web (with help of course), the defining of HTML (hypertext markup language) used to create web pages, HTTP (HyperText Transfer Protocol) and URLs (Universal Resource Locators). All of those developments took place between 1989 and 1991.

- Tim Berners-Lee was born in London, England and graduated in Physics from Oxford University in 1976. He is currently the Director of the World Wide Web Consortium, the group that sets technical standards for the Web.

1991

The digital answering machine invented.
- Dr. Kazuo Hashimoto of Japan invented the digital answering machine in 1983, but it wasn't until 1991 that they were commercially produced and available all over the US. founder Scott A. Jones invented voicemail in 1987.

1992

The smart pill invented.
- Gregory Pincus and Min Chueh Chang are credited with the invention of the birth control pill. Both were biologists whose research with fertility led to the discovery that ovulation

1993

The pentium processor invented.
- In 1993, Intel announced the Pentium chip. The word "Pentium" comes from the Greek root word "pentas" meaning "five." The Pentium is

the Intel 80586 chip. The Pentium is a 32-bit chip with superscalar design, and is estimated to be two times faster than the 486DX2 (66MHz) chip. The Pentium uses dual pipelines to allow it to process two separate instructions in a single cycle. The Pentium has a 64 bit bus interface, an eight bit code cache, an eight bit data cache, and branch prediction memory bank. Don Alpert was the architecture manager of the Pentium, John Crawford was co-manager. In March 1994, Intel announced new and faster versions of the Pentium microprocessor, with speeds of over 100 MHz. By 1996, 200 Mhz microcomputer systems were available on the market. (This chip has now been far surpassed by current microprocessor technology.)

1994

HIV protease inhibitor invented.

- Ritonavir, a peptidomimetic HIV protease inhibitor, was marketed in 1996. It was designed to fit the C2-symmetry in the binding site of the protease. The developers of ritonavir, Abbott Laboratories, started with compounds that were active against the virus but had poor bioavailability. Some improvements were made, for example the terminal phenyl residues were removed and pyridyl groups put instead to add water solubility. The final product of these improvements was ritonavir. Significant gastrointestinal side effects and a large pill burden are ritonavir's main drawbacks and is therefore not used as a single treatment. However, it is a strong inhibitor of the cytochrome P450 enzyme mediated metabolism and it is only used in a combination therapy with other protease inhibitors for pharmacokinetic boosting.

1995

The Java computer language invented.
- On 23 May 1995, John Gage, the director of the Science Office of the Sun Microsystems along with Marc Andreesen, co-founder and executive vice president at Netscape announced to an audience of SunWorldTM that Java technology wasn't a myth and that it was a reality and that it was going to be incorporated into Netscape Navigator.
- At the time the total number of people working on Java was less than 30. This team would shape the future in the next decade and no one had any idea as to what was in store. From being the mind of an unmanned vehicle on Mars to the operating environment on most of the consumer electronics, e.g. cable set-top boxes,

VCRs, toasters and also for personal digital assistants (PDAs)

DVD (Digital Versatile Disc or Digital Video Disc) invented.
•   DVD as an industry standard was announced in November 1995 and backed by major players in the CE, IT and movie industry. The first players appeared in Japan in November, 1996, followed by U.S. players in March, 1997. To produce DVD players, one needs to license a range of patents, owned by different companies. A number of these companies (Philips, Sony, Matsushita and Toshiba) have decided to license the necessary patents through one licensing agent. Philips has been selected to take up this administrative role. Matshusita, was the company mainly responsible for the development of DVD as it is today. Philips, one of the first companies to make CD players, was the first to make a DVD player. The invention of DVD cannot be attributed to one person or one company.

1996

Web TV invented.
•   The technology of WebTV was developed by Diba Inc and Zenith Electronics in 1996.

Subsequently, Zenith Electronics produced and marketed the first WebTV sets.

1997

The gas-powered fuel cell invented.
• October 23, 1997, Arthur D. Little invented the gas-powered fuel cell. The new technology promises greater fuel efficiencies, near-zero emission levels, and lower cost fuel alternatives for the automobile industry.

1998

Viagra invented.
• The diamond shaped blue pill Viagra, which is responsible for giving a whole new perception of sexuality to the modern society, has a similarly interesting history behind its invention. The inventors of Viagra actually wanted to invent a medicine for the cure of cardio-vascular diseases, but fortunately or unfortunately, they developed a medicine which could reverse impotence or erectile dysfunction for the first time.

1999

Scientists measure the fastest wind speed ever recorded on earth, 509 km/h(318 mph).

- Scientists have measured a wind speed of 318 mph (509km/h) inside a tornado that recently struck Oklahoma City - the fastest wind speed ever recorded on Earth.
- Until recently it was not thought that such a wind speed was possible.
- The previous fastest measured speed was 286 mph (458 km/h). That was also measured in a tornado in Oklahoma.
- The fastest non-tornado wind ever recorded was is 231 mph (370 km/h), measured at Mount Washington in New Hampshire in 1934.
- By comparison, the wind that ravaged the southern part of the United Kingdom in October 1987 was estimated to be less than 100 mph (160 km/h).

There doesn't seem to be too many inventions during the 90's. However, many of these were technically invented, to some degree, before actually being known.

Somebody once said that there is nothing new under the sun. It's just the way we put things together that makes them new.

Inventions & Events

1990 - 1999 - Events

1990

Hubble Telescope Launched Into Space
- On April 24th, 1990, the Space Shuttle mission that would deploy the Hubble Space Telescope launched into space.
- The telescope has a 94.5 inch mirror and is expected to look deeper into space and with a clarity 10 times greater than ever achieved by an earth-based telescope. The telescope is projected to be operational for 10-15 years with periodic servicing by astronauts via the shuttle.
- The project had been in the works for 12 years and was deployed seven years after its original launch date. The delay in the launch date was only the beginning of the problems the Hubble space telescope was to encounter. Besides being launched late and millions of dollars over budget, the telescope has had serious problems since being deployed, the first being the miscalculations in the design of the telescope's lens. This was not discovered until the telescope was in space; thus it was necessary for the space shuttle to conduct a mission repairing the design problems and consequently costing the taxpay-

er even more money for the project and delaying its use.

Lech Walesa Becomes First President of Poland

- In 1988, deteriorating economic conditions led to a new wave of labor strikes across Poland, and the government was forced to negotiate with Walesa. In April 1989, Solidarity was again legalized, and its members were allowed to enter a limited number of candidates in upcoming elections. By September, a Solidarity-led government coalition was in place, with Walesa's colleague Tadeusz Mazowiecki as premier. In 1990, Poland's first direct presidential election was held, and Walesa won by a landslide.
- President Walesa successfully implemented free-market reforms, but unfortunately he was a far more effective labor leader than president. In 1995, he was narrowly defeated in his reelection by former communist Aleksander Kwasniewski, head of the Democratic Left Alliance.

Nelson Mandela Freed

- Mandela spent the first 18 of his 27 years in jail at the brutal Robben Island Prison. Confined to a small cell without a bed or plumbing, he was forced to do hard labor in a quarry. He could write and receive a letter once every six

months, and once a year he was allowed to meet with a visitor for 30 minutes. However, Mandela's resolve remained unbroken, and while remaining the symbolic leader of the anti-apartheid movement, he led a movement of civil disobedience at the prison that coerced South African officials into drastically improving conditions on Robben Island. He was later moved to another location, where he lived under house arrest.
- In 1989, F.W. de Klerk became South African president and set about dismantling apartheid. De Klerk lifted the ban on the ANC, suspended executions, and in February 1990 ordered the release of Nelson Mandela.
- Mandela subsequently led the ANC in its negotiations with the minority government for an end to apartheid and the establishment of a multiracial government. In 1993, Mandela and de Klerk were jointly awarded the Nobel Peace Prize. One year later, the ANC won an electoral majority in the country's first free elections, and Mandela was elected South Africa's president.

U.S. President Bush Announces That He Doesn't Like Broccoli

- President Bush declared today that he never, ever, wants to see another sprig of broccoli on his plate, whether he is on Air Force One

or at the White House or anywhere else in the land.
- "I do not like broccoli," the President said, responding to queries about a broccoli ban he has imposed aboard Air Force One, first reported this week in U.S. News and World Report. "And I haven't liked it since I was a little kid and my mother made me eat it. And I'm President of the United States, and I'm not going to eat any more broccoli!"

Devastating new currency law goes into effect July 1st, 2014.
- FATCA requires foreign financial institutions (FFI) of broad scope - banks, stock brokers, hedge funds, pension funds, insurance companies, trusts - to report directly to the IRS all clients' accounts owned by U.S. Citizens and U.S. persons (Green Card holders).
- Starting July 1, 2014, FATCA will require FFIs to provide annual reports to the Internal Revenue Service (IRS) on the name and address of each U.S. client, as well as the largest account balance in the year and total debits and credits of any account owned by a U.S. person.

1991

Collapse of the Soviet Union

- In December of 1991, as the world watched in amazement, the Soviet Union disintegrated into fifteen separate countries. Its collapse was hailed by the west as a victory for freedom, a triumph of democracy over totalitarianism, and evidence of the superiority of capitalism over socialism. The United States rejoiced as its formidable enemy was brought to its knees, thereby ending the Cold War which had hovered over these two superpowers since the end of World War II. Indeed, the breakup of the Soviet Union transformed the entire world political situation, leading to a complete reformulation of political, economic and military alliances all over the globe.
- What led to this monumental historical event? In fact, the answer is a very complex one, and can only be arrived at with an understanding of the peculiar composition and history of the Soviet Union. The Soviet Union was built on approximately the same territory as the Russian Empire which it succeeded. After the Bolshevik Revolution of 1917, the newly-formed government developed a philosophy of socialism with the eventual and gradual transition to Communism. The state which the Bolsheviks created was intended to overcome national differences, and rather to create one monolithic state based on a cen-

tralized economical and political system. This state, which was built on a Communist ideology, was eventually transformed into a totalitarian state, in which the Communist leadership had complete control over the country.
- However, this project of creating a unified, centralized socialist state proved problematic for several reasons. First, the Soviets underestimated the degree to which the non-Russian ethnic groups in the country (which comprised more than fifty percent of the total population of the Soviet Union) would resist assimilation into a Russianized State. Second, their economic planning failed to meet the needs of the State, which was caught up in a vicious arms race with the United States. This led to gradual economic decline, eventually necessitating the need for reform. Finally, the ideology of Communism, which the Soviet Government worked to instill in the hearts and minds of its population, never took firm root, and eventually lost whatever influence it had originally carried.

Copper Age Man Found Frozen in Glacier
- On September 19, 1991, two German tourists were hiking in the Otzal Alps near the Italian-Austrian border when they discovered Europe's oldest known mummy sticking out of the ice. Otzi, as the Iceman is now known, had

been naturally mummified by the ice and kept in amazing condition for approximately 5,300 years. Research on Otzi's preserved body and the various artifacts found with it continues to reveal much about the life of Copper Age Europeans.

Operation Desert Storm
- "Soldiers, sailors, airmen and Marines of the United States Central Command, this morning at 0300, we launched Operation DESERT STORM, an offensive campaign that will enforce the United Nation's resolutions that Iraq must cease its rape and pillage of its weaker neighbor and withdraw its forces from Kuwait. My confidence in you is total. Our cause is just! Now you must be the thunder and lightning of Desert Storm. May God be with you, your loved ones at home, and our Country." -- General H. Norman Schwarzkopf, USA Commander-in-Chief U.S. Central Command, in a message to the command, 16 January 1991

South Africa Repeals Apartheid Laws
- The vote on 17 June 1991 that repealed the legal framework of Apartheid and began the process that would eventually abolish Apartheid as a whole was bitterly contested as many members of the White electorate sought to cling

to the privileges afforded to them under Apartheid. The legal framework in question, consisting of four Acts, namely, the Population Registration Act of 1950, The Group Areas Act, the Land Act and the Separate Amenities Act.
- The repealing of these Acts did not include extending the right to vote to all of South Africa's citizens. FW de Klerk, who was President at the time, committed himself to this eventuality as soon as a new constitution was drafted. This process culminated in the first democratic elections in 1994, with Nelson Mandela as the first Black President. The repeal of the legal framework was the result of unified opposition by people from all over the world, who collectively put pressure on the Apartheid government, lobbied for sanctions, and supported the work of the liberation movements and civil society in exposing the evils of the Apartheid system.

1992

Official End of the Cold War
- The Cold War period of 1985–1991 began with the rise of Mikhail Gorbachev as leader of the Soviet Union. Gorbachev was a revolutionary leader for the USSR, as he was the first to promote liberalization of the political landscape (Glasnost) and capitalist elements into the

economy (Perestroika); prior to this, the USSR had been strictly prohibiting liberal reform and maintained an inefficient centralized economy. The USSR, facing massive economic difficulties, was also greatly interested in reducing the costly arms race with the U.S. President Ronald Reagan, although peaceful confrontation and arms buildups throughout much of his term prevented the USSR from cutting back its military spending as much as it might have liked. Regardless, the USSR began to crumble as liberal reforms proved difficult to handle and capitalist changes to the centralized economy were badly transitioned and caused major problems. After a series of revolutions in Soviet Bloc states, and a failed coup by conservative elements opposed to the ongoing reforms, the Soviet Union collapsed in 1991.

Riots in Los Angeles After the Rodney King Verdict

- The "Rodney King Riots," also known as the "Los Angeles Riots," began April 29, 1992, after four Los Angeles Police Department (LAPD) officers were acquitted of charges in the savage beating of Rodney King (pictured below). The racially sparked riots lasted more than six days, with thousands of Angelenos taking to the streets in an especially violent display of protest. Fifty-three people were killed and more than two thousand were said to be injured.

1993

Cult Compound in Waco, Texas Raided

- After hearing reports that Branch Davidian cult leader David Koresh had been abusing children and amassing a store of weapons, the Bureau of Alcohol, Tobacco and Firearms (ATF) gathered resources and planned to raid the Branch Davidian compound, known as the Mount Carmel Center located just outside of Waco, Texas. With a warrant to search for illegal firearms in hand, the ATF attempted to storm the compound on February 28, 1993.
- A gunfight ensued (debate continues over which side fired the first shot). The shooting lasted nearly two hours, leaving four ATF agents and five Branch Davidians dead.
- For 51 days, the ATF and the FBI waited outside the compound, using negotiators to try to end the stand-off peacefully. (There has been much criticism as to how the government handled the negotiations.)
- Although a number of children and a few adults were released during this period, 84 men, women, and children stayed in the compound.

- On April 19, 1993, the ATF and FBI attempted to end the siege by using a form of tear gas (called CS gas), a decision approved by US Attorney General Janet Reno. Early in the morning, specialized tank-like vehicles (Combat Engineering Vehicles) punctured holes in the compound's walls and inserted CS gas. The government was hoping that the gas would safely push the Branch Davidians out of the compound.
- In response to the gas, the Branch Davidians shot back. Just after noon, the wooden compound caught on fire.
- While nine people escaped the blaze, 75 perished either by gunshot or by fire inside the compound. Twenty-five of the dead were children. Koresh was also found dead, from a gunshot wound to the head.

Lorena Bobbitt Takes Brutal Revenge
- On the night of June 23, 1993, 26-year-old John Wayne Bobbitt came home to his Manassas, Virginia apartment after a night out partying and drinking. According to his wife, Lorena Bobbitt, John then raped her.
- The couple had already been married for four years and during that time, Lorena had allegedly suffered from years of emotional, physical, and sexual abuse by John. John also frequently boasted about his infidelities and had forced

Lorena to have an abortion. All this built up to this particular night, when Lorena finally snapped.
- While John was asleep, Lorena got out of bed and went into the kitchen for a drink of water. While in the kitchen, she saw an eight-inch carving knife sitting on the counter. Lorena grabbed the knife, then walked back to the bedroom where John was sleeping. She pulled back the covers and then sliced John Bobbitt's penis nearly in half.
- In a daze, Lorena got into her car and started heading to her work, while still holding both the knife and the severed penis. After driving for a little while, she rolled down her car window and threw the severed penis out the window. It landed in an empty field.
- Shortly thereafter, Lorena realized, at least partly, the severity of her actions and called 911. John was rushed to a hospital in the hopes of stopping the bleeding. After an extensive search by police, John's severed penis was found, packed in ice, and also rushed to the hospital. After nine hours of surgery, John Bobbitt's penis was reattached.

Use of the Internet Grows Exponentially

- Internet Traffic has doubled every 100 days. In 1994, a mere 3 million people were

connected to the Internet. By the end of 1997, more than 100 million were using it.
- Faster Growth - The Internet is growing faster than all other technologies that have preceded it.
- Radio existed for 38 years before it had 50 million listeners, and television took 13 years to reach that mark. The Internet crossed the line in just four years.
- Internet Commerce and business will likely surpass US$300 billion by 2002. Using credit cards, 10 million people in the United States and Canada had purchased something on the WWW by the end of 1997, an increase from 4.7 million people six months earlier.

World Trade Center Bombed

- At 12:18 p.m., a terrorist bomb explodes in a parking garage of the World Trade Center in New York City, leaving a crater 60 feet wide and causing the collapse of several steel-reinforced concrete floors in the vicinity of the blast. Although the terrorist bomb failed to critically damage the main structure of the skyscrapers, six people were killed and more than 1,000 were injured. The World Trade Center itself suffered more than $500 million in damage. After the attack, authorities evacuated 50,000 people from the buildings, hundreds of whom were suf-

fering from smoke inhalation. The evacuation lasted the whole afternoon.
- City authorities and the Federal Bureau of Investigation (FBI) undertook a massive manhunt for suspects, and within days several radical Islamic fundamentalists were arrested. In March 1994, Mohammed Salameh, Ahmad Ajaj, Nidal Ayyad, and Mahmoud Abouhalima were convicted by a federal jury for their role in the bombing, and each was sentenced to life in prison. Salameh, a Palestinian, was arrested when he went to retrieve the $400 deposit he had left for the Ryder rental van used in the attack. Ajaj and Ayyad, who both played a role in the construction of the bomb, were arrested soon after. Abouhalima, who helped buy and mix the explosives, fled to Saudi Arabia but was caught in Egypt two weeks later.
- The mastermind of the attack--Ramzi Ahmed Yousef--remained at large until February 1995, when he was arrested in Pakistan. He had previously been in the Philippines, and in a computer he left there were found terrorist plans that included a plot to kill Pope John Paul II and a plan to bomb 15 American airliners in 48 hours. On the flight back to the United States, Yousef reportedly admitted to a Secret Service agent that he had directed the Trade Center attack from the beginning and even claimed to have

set the fuse that exploded the 1,200-pound bomb. His only regret, the agent quoted Yousef saying, was that the 110-story tower did not collapse into its twin as planned--a catastrophe that would have caused thousands of deaths.
- Eyad Ismoil, who drove the Ryder van into the parking garage below the World Trade Center, was captured in Jordan that year and taken back to New York. All the men implicated had ties to Sheik Omar Abdel Rahman, a radical Egyptian religious leader who operated out of Jersey City, New Jersey, located just across the Hudson River from Manhattan. In 1995, Rahman and 10 followers were convicted of conspiring to blow up the United Nations headquarters and other New York landmarks. Prosecutors argued that the World Trade Center attack was part of that conspiracy, though little clear evidence of this charge was presented.
- In November 1997, Yousef and Ismoil were convicted in a courtroom only a few blocks away from the twin towers and subsequently sentenced to life in prison without the possibility of parole. Only one other man believed to be directly involved in the attack, Iraqi Abdul Rahman Yasin, remains at large.

1994

Channel Tunnel Opens, Connecting Britain and France

- On May 6, 1994, the Channel Tunnel, also known as the Chunnel, officially opened. The Channel Tunnel is a set of three 31.25-mile long tunnels that connect the island of Great Britain to the mainland of France. The Channel Tunnel, which took six years and over $15 billion to construct, is considered one of the greatest feats of engineering of the 20th century.

Nelson Mandela Elected President of South Africa

- Nelson Mandela has become South Africa's first black president after more than three centuries of white rule.
- Mr Mandela's African National Congress (ANC) party won 252 of the 400 seats in the first democratic elections of South Africa's history.
- The inauguration ceremony took place in the Union Buildings amphitheatre in Pretoria today, attended by politicians and dignitaries from more than 140 countries around the world.
- Never, never again will this beautiful land experience the oppression of one by another, Nelson Mandela

O.J. Simpson Arrested for Double Murder

- June 17, 1994: Orenthal James (O.J.) Simpson is arrested for a double murder. Nicole Brown Simpson and Ronald Goldman were brutally murdered outside Nicole's apartment on June 12, 1994. Both victims were repeatedly stabbed and both had defensive wounds, attesting to their struggle in the attack. The Simpsons had been divorced for two years at the time of the murders. Their two children were asleep inside the apartment. The relationship between Nicole and Goldman has never been clearly defined. Evidence at the scene of the crime led police to suspect O.J.
- O.J. had gained fame as a football star with the NFL as a running back. After his football career ended, he became a spokesman for a car rental agency and ran through airports and jumped over obstacles to get to his waiting car. He became an actor and was recognized across the country, if not the world. Police permitted him to turn himself in, thinking he was not a flight risk. O.J. was to be at the police station at 11 AM on this date. He didn't show.
- At 2 PM, the police issued an all-points bulletin for O.J. His lawyer and friend read a disjointed and confusing letter from the ex-football star that sounded like a suicide note. The police tracked cellular phone calls to find Simpson.

They found his friend, Al Cowlings, driving a white Ford Bronco heading south on Interstate 405. When police approached the SUV, Cowlings told them O.J. was in the back seat, holding a gun to his own head. Police backed away.
- Police followed the white Bronco down the freeway at speeds of only 35 mph. At the beginning of the low-speed chase, a lone helicopter flew above and filmed the event. As the pursuit continued, other film crews took to the air and radio announcers pleaded with O.J. to give himself up. The roadway was cleared of traffic and the country watched as a phalanx of police cruisers paced the SUV. The chase ended at 8 PM when O.J. was taken into custody outside his home.

Rwandan Genocide
- Rwandan armed forces kill 10 Belgian peacekeeping officers in a successful effort to discourage international intervention in their genocide that had begun only hours earlier. In less than three months, Hutu extremists who controlled Rwanda murdered an estimated 800,000 innocent civilian Tutsis in the worst episode of genocide since World War II. The Tutsis, a minority group that made up about 10 percent of Rwanda's population, received no assistance from the international community, al-

though the United Nations later conceded that a mere 5,000 soldiers deployed at the outset would have stopped the wholesale slaughter.

1995

Sarin Gas Attack in Tokyo Subway

- On Monday, March 20, 1995, five members of the Aum Shinrikyo religious cult boarded separate subway trains in Tokyo. Each cult member carried either two or three bags of sarin in liquid form, tightly enclosed in plastic, and then wrapped in newspapers. Each also carried an umbrella.
- Around 8 a.m., the cult members dropped their packages onto the floor of the trains, then used the sharp end of their umbrellas to puncture holes through the plastic. As the liquid poured out of the holes, it seeped onto the train floors and started to turn into toxic sarin gas.
- The cult members then exited their subway trains and were picked up in pre-arranged getaway cars, leaving the sarin gas, estimated to be 500 times more potent than cyanide gas, to dissipate among the passengers that remained in the subway.

Oklahoma City Bombing
- At 9:02 a.m. on April 19, 1995, a 5,000-pound bomb, hidden inside a Ryder truck, exploded just outside the Alfred P. Murrah Federal Building in Oklahoma City. The explosion caused massive damage to the building and killed 168 people, 19 of whom were children. Those responsible for what became known as the Oklahoma City Bombing were home-grown terrorists, Timothy McVeigh and Terry Nichols. This deadly bombing was the worst terrorist attack on U.S. soil until the September 11, 2001 World Trade Center attack.

Yitzhak Rabin Assassinated
- Israeli Prime Minister Yitzhak Rabin is fatally shot after attending a peace rally held in Tel Aviv's Kings Square in Israel. Rabin later died in surgery at Ichilov Hospital in Tel Aviv.
- The 73-year-old prime minister was walking to his car when he was shot in the arm and the back by Yigal Amir, a 27-year-old Jewish law student who had connections to the far-right Jewish group Eyal. Israeli police arrested Amir at the scene of the shooting, and he later confessed to the assassination, explaining at his arraignment that he killed Rabin because the prime minister wanted "to give our country to the Arabs."

- Born in Jerusalem, Rabin was a leader of the Arab-Israeli war of 1948 and served as chief-of-staff of Israel's armed forces during the Six-Day War of 1967. After serving as Israel's ambassador to the United States, Rabin entered the Labour Party and became prime minister in 1974. As prime minister, he conducted the negotiations that resulted in a 1974 cease-fire with Syria and the 1975 military disengagement agreement between Israel and Egypt. In 1977, Rabin resigned as prime minister over a scandal involving his holding of bank accounts in the United States in violation of Israeli law. From 1984 to 1990, he served as his country's defense minister.
- In 1992, Rabin led the Labour Party to election victory and became Israel's prime minister again. In 1993, he signed the historic Israeli-Palestinian Declaration of Principles with Palestinian leader Yasir Arafat and in 1994 concluded a formal peace agreement with the Palestinians. In October 1994, Rabin and Arafat shared the Nobel Peace Prize, along with Israeli foreign minister Shimon Peres. One year later, Rabin was assassinated. Peres succeeded him as prime minister.

1996

Mad Cow Disease Hits Britain

- London: British scientists have detected a previously unknown brain condition that caused paralysis and death in a young cow, officials said yesterday in a potential new blow to an industry hit by mad cow disease.
- An investigation was begun after white material was found on the brain of a heifer that died after suffering paralysis for about six days, the Department for Environment and Rural Affairs said.
- "The Veterinary Laboratories Agency have recorded possibly a new condition in cattle in the UK," a spokesman said. "In layman's terms, a type of cattle polio was identified which we haven't seen before."
- A series of diseases have already been ruled out, including louping-ill, a virus transmitted by ticks that causes inflammation of the brain and spinal cord.
- It was too soon to say whether there was any potential risk to humans, the spokesman said. "The long-term risk to public health is not known. It is impossible to make an assessment from a single case where the agent responsible is not known."
- Britain's beef industry has been severely hit since cases of the human form of mad cow disease, or bovine spongiform encephalopathy, were first detected in 1996.

Two Royal Divorces
- It was 15 years ago on Aug. 28, 1996, that the divorce of Prince Charles and Princess Diana became official. After four years of separation, the fairy tale that began with their wedding in 1981 ended in divorce for the most-watched royal couple. A year later, Princess Diana died in Paris in a tragic car accident.
- Sarah Ferguson married Prince Andrew July 23, 1986, at Westminster Abbey. They had two daughters together who are nephews of Prince Charles and cousins to Prince William. People magazine reported in 1992 the couple separated after she was found cheating on him. The divorce was finalized in 1996. The Daily Mail reported in 2010 that Ferguson sought more money from her ex-husband beyond their original divorce settlement. Her secretly recorded statements caused a scandal in Britain.

Unabomber Arrested
- On April 3rd, at his small wilderness cabin near Lincoln, Montana, Theodore John Kaczynski is arrested by FBI agents and accused of being the Unabomber, the elusive terrorist blamed for 16 mail bombs that killed three people and injured 23 during an 18-year period.

1997

British Au Pair on Trial for Murder
- Louise Woodward, the British au pair who was jailed for the shaking death of 8-month old American Matthew Eappen in 1997, has just given birth to her own baby girl on New Year's Day, according to the Birmingham Mail.
- Woodward was sentenced to 15 years in prison by a Boston court for second-degree murder, but she only served 279 days when an appeals court upheld the judge's decision to downgrade the charge to manslaughter.
- Judge Hiller Zobel said he believed Woodward had acted out of "confusion, inexperience, frustration, immaturity and some anger, but not malice in the legal sense."

Hale-Bopp Comet Visible
- Comet Hale–Bopp (formally designated C/1995 O1) was perhaps the most widely observed comet of the 20th century and one of the brightest seen for many decades. It was visible to the naked eye for a record 18 months, twice as long as the previous record holder, the Great Comet of 1811.
- Hale–Bopp was discovered on July 23, 1995, at a great distance from the Sun, raising expecta-

tions that the comet would brighten considerably by the time it passed close to Earth. Although predicting the brightness of comets with any degree of accuracy is very difficult, Hale–Bopp met or exceeded most predictions when it passed perihelion on April 1, 1997. The comet was dubbed the Great Comet of 1997.

Hong Kong Returned to China

- At midnight on July 1, 1997, Hong Kong reverts back to Chinese rule in a ceremony attended by British Prime Minister Tony Blair, Prince Charles of Wales, Chinese President Jiang Zemin, and U.S. Secretary of State Madeleine Albright. A few thousand Hong Kongers protested the turnover, which was otherwise celebratory and peaceful.
- In 1839, Britain invaded China to crush opposition to its interference in the country's economic, social, and political affairs. One of Britain's first acts of the war was to occupy Hong Kong, a sparsely inhabited island off the coast of southeast China. In 1841, China ceded the island to the British with the signing of the Convention of Chuenpi, and in 1842 the Treaty of Nanking was signed, formally ending the First Opium War.
- Britain's new colony flourished as an East-West trading center and as the commercial gateway and distribution center for southern China. In

1898, Britain was granted an additional 99 years of rule over Hong Kong under the Second Convention of Peking. In September 1984, after years of negotiations, the British and the Chinese signed a formal agreement approving the 1997 turnover of the island in exchange for a Chinese pledge to preserve Hong Kong's capitalist system. On July 1, 1997, Hong Kong was peaceably handed over to China in a ceremony attended by numerous Chinese, British, and international dignitaries. The chief executive under the new Hong Kong government, Tung Chee Hwa, formulated a policy based on the concept of "one country, two systems," thus preserving Hong Kong's role as a principal capitalist center in Asia.

Pathfinder Sends Back Images of Mars

- PASADENA, California (CNN) -- The Mars Pathfinder space probe sent back the first panoramic color images of the desolate, rock-strewn surface of Mars Friday evening.
- The first red-tinged views of the planet from Pathfinder, perched amidst the rocky Martian floor, were released by NASA about 9:35 p.m. EDT (0135 GMT) -- less than nine hours after the spacecraft made a landing that one NASA scientist described as "way beyond our expectations."

Princess Diana Dies in Car Crash
- On August 31, 1997, Diana, Princess of Wales died after being involved in a car accident. Diana had been riding in the Mercedes-Benz with her boyfriend (Dodi Al Fayed), bodyguard (Trevor Rees-Jones), and chauffer (Henri Paul) when the car crashed into a pillar of the tunnel under the Pont de l'Alma bridge in Paris while fleeing from paparazzi.
- Dodi Al Fayed and Henri Paul were pronounced dead at the scene. Diana and Trevor Rees-Jones were taken to the hospital. Diana had suffered major injuries, including to her head and chest. Diana died on the operating table. Trevor, though severely injured, survived the accident.

Scientists Clone Sheep
- Scientists in Scotland have announced the birth of the world's first successfully cloned mammal, Dolly the sheep.
- Dolly, who was created at the Roslin Institute in Edinburgh, was actually born on 5 July 1996 although her arrival has only just been revealed.
- Dolly is the first mammal to have been successfully cloned from an adult cell. Previous clonings have been from embryo cells.

Tallest Buildings in the World Built in Kuala Lumpur
- The Petronas Twin Towers in Kuala Lumpur, Malaysia, were the world's tallest buildings from 1998 to 2004, and are still the tallest twin buildings. Chicago's Willis Tower (originally the Sears Tower) was the tallest building in the world from 1974 to 1998.

Tiger Woods Wins Masters
- April 13, Tiger Woods, whose father is African-American and mother is Thai, becomes the first person of color to win the Masters at Augusta National Golf Club, which admitted its first black member in 1990.

1998

India and Pakistan Test Nuclear Weapons
- India's and Pakistan's recent nuclear weapons tests have demonstrated to the world that both have bombs. The Prime Minister's Office stated: "These tests have established that India has a proven capability for a weaponised nuclear programme." J. N. Dixit, formerly India's Foreign Secretary, added that "by conducting these tests, which included a thermo-nuclear device, India has affirmed to itself and con-

firmed to the world its status as a full-fledged nuclear weapon state."
- It is also clear that the bombs are deliverable. Arguments about preventing India and Pakistan from weaponizing or deploying their weapons appear to be off the mark - the bombs could be dropped tomorrow. According to Mr. Dixit, "India has already weaponised itself in terms of various warhead manufacturing capacities and delivery systems. The question to be asked is whether we should move on to deployment of these capacities. I make a distinction between actual deployment and deployability." Furthermore, an Indian official from Prime Minister's office said, "if you're asking me if we have a delivery system, the answer is yes we do."

Titanic Most Successful Movie Ever

- The year is 1997 and Titanic the movie is released in America on December 19.
- Titanic becomes the most successful film ever to be released.
- James Cameron is credited with writing and directing this romantic drama while 20th Century Fox took on the role of distributing it to box offices everywhere. Paramount Pictures also supplied some funding.
- This version of Titanic was definitely entertaining but was it based on reality?

- How much investment capital was risked in bringing Titanic to the big screen ?
- This Cameron project begins in the mid 1990's when the film maker starts shooting footage of the actual RMS Titanic which is lying at the bottom of the North Atlantic ocean. The Royal Merchant Ship Titanic was located in 1985 .
- For Cameron to complete his Titanic movie, which he intended to release in July of 1997, he built a modest replica of the original ocean liner. He also had designer and computer animators build scaled models and computer animated models.
- When Cameron pitched the Titanic idea to the intended producer he mentioned the sum of 150 million dollars as the investment cost.
- There was more than 200 million dollars involved in the production of Titanic but most reviews claim that Titanic, the most successful movie ever made to that point, went way over this budget.

U.S. President Clinton Impeached

- After nearly 14 hours of debate, the House of Representatives approves two articles of impeachment against President Bill Clinton, charging him with lying under oath to a federal grand jury and obstructing justice. Clinton, the second

president in American history to be impeached, vowed to finish his term.
- In November 1995, Clinton began an affair with Monica Lewinsky, a 21-year-old unpaid intern. Over the course of a year and a half, the president and Lewinsky had nearly a dozen sexual encounters in the White House. In April 1996, Lewinsky was transferred to the Pentagon. That summer, she first confided in Pentagon co-worker Linda Tripp about her sexual relationship with the president. In 1997, with the relationship over, Tripp began secretly to record conversations with Lewinsky, in which Lewinsky gave Tripp details about the affair.
- In December, lawyers for Paula Jones, who was suing the president on sexual harassment charges, subpoenaed Lewinsky. In January 1998, allegedly under the recommendation of the president, Lewinsky filed an affidavit in which she denied ever having had a sexual relationship with him. Five days later, Tripp contacted the office of Kenneth Starr, the Whitewater independent counsel, to talk about Lewinsky and the tapes she made of their conversations. Tripp, wired by FBI agents working with Starr, met with Lewinsky again, and on January 16, Lewinsky was taken by FBI agents and U.S. attorneys to a hotel room where she was questioned and offered immunity if she cooperated

with the prosecution. A few days later, the story broke, and Clinton publicly denied the allegations, saying, "I did not have sexual relations with that woman, Ms. Lewinsky."
- In late July, lawyers for Lewinsky and Starr worked out a full-immunity agreement covering both Lewinsky and her parents, all of whom Starr had threatened with prosecution. On August 6, Lewinsky appeared before the grand jury to begin her testimony, and on August 17 President Clinton testified. Contrary to his testimony in the Paula Jones sexual-harassment case, President Clinton acknowledged to prosecutors from the office of the independent counsel that he had had an extramarital affair with Ms. Lewinsky.
- In four hours of closed-door testimony, conducted in the Map Room of the White House, Clinton spoke live via closed-circuit television to a grand jury in a nearby federal courthouse. He was the first sitting president ever to testify before a grand jury investigating his conduct. That evening, President Clinton also gave a four-minute televised address to the nation in which he admitted he had engaged in an inappropriate relationship with Lewinsky. In the brief speech, which was wrought with legalisms, the word "sex" was never spoken, and the word "regret"

was used only in reference to his admission that he misled the public and his family.
- Less than a month later, on September 9, Kenneth Starr submitted his report and 18 boxes of supporting documents to the House of Representatives. Released to the public two days later, the Starr Report outlined a case for impeaching Clinton on 11 grounds, including perjury, obstruction of justice, witness-tampering, and abuse of power, and also provided explicit details of the sexual relationship between the president and Ms. Lewinsky. On October 8, the House authorized a wide-ranging impeachment inquiry, and on December 11, the House Judiciary Committee approved three articles of impeachment. On December 19, the House impeached Clinton.
- On January 7, 1999, in a congressional procedure not seen since the 1868 impeachment trial of President Andrew Johnson, the trial of President Clinton got underway in the Senate. As instructed in Article 1 of the U.S. Constitution, the chief justice of the U.S. Supreme Court (William Rehnquist at this time) was sworn in to preside, and the senators were sworn in as jurors.
- Five weeks later, on February 12, the Senate voted on whether to remove Clinton from office. The president was acquitted on both articles of impeachment. The prosecution needed a two-

thirds majority to convict but failed to achieve even a bare majority. Rejecting the first charge of perjury, 45 Democrats and 10 Republicans voted "not guilty," and on the charge of obstruction of justice the Senate was split 50-50. After the trial concluded, President Clinton said he was "profoundly sorry" for the burden his behavior imposed on Congress and the American people.

1999

The Euro the New European Currency
- Euro becomes official currency in the eleven participating countries. The definition and execution of the single monetary policy in euro commences. Foreign exchange operations are beginning to be carried out in euro. New public debt is issued in euro; old public debt will be translated into euro. Stocks and bonds will be quoted in euro on all stock exchanges in the member area. National currencies will simply be denominations of the euro, and continue to be used as a matter of convenience only until 2002.

Fear of Y2K Bug
- While many were ready to party "like it was 1999," many others predicted catastrophe at the

end of the year from a small assumption made long ago when computers were first being programmed.
- The Y2K (Year 2000) problem existed because most dates in computers were programmed to automatically assume the date began with "19" as in "1977" and "1988." But when the date was to turn from December 31, 1999 to January 1, 2000, it was prophesied that computers would be so confused that they would shut down completely.

JFK Jr. Dies in Plane Accident
- On July 16, 1999, John F. Kennedy, Jr.; his wife, Carolyn Bessette Kennedy; and her sister, Lauren Bessette, die when the single-engine plane that Kennedy was piloting crashes into the Atlantic Ocean near Martha's Vineyard, Massachusetts.

Killing Spree at Columbine High School
- April 20, 1999, two teenage gunmen kill 13 people in a shooting spree at Columbine High School in Littleton, Colorado, south of Denver. At approximately 11:19 a.m., Dylan Klebold, 18, and Eric Harris, 17, dressed in trench coats, began shooting students outside the school before moving inside to continue their rampage. By 11:35 a.m., Klebold and Harris had killed 12 fel-

low students and a teacher and wounded another 23 people. Shortly after noon, the two teens turned their guns on themselves and committed suicide.

NATO Attacks Serbia
- The NATO bombing marked the second major combat operation in its history, following the 1995 NATO bombing campaign in Bosnia and Herzegovina. The 1999 bombings led to the withdrawal of Yugoslav forces from Kosovo, the establishment of UNMIK, a U.N. mission in Kosovo and put an end to the Yugoslav Wars of the 1990s.

Panama Canal Returns to Panama
- From 1979 to 1999, a bi-national transitional Panama Canal Commission ran the canal, with an American leader for the first decade and a Panamanian administrator for the second. The transition at the end of 1999 was very smooth, for over 90% of the canal employees were Panamanian by 1996.

Inventions & Events

Inventions & Events

Geo. W. Bush - 2000 - 2008

2000 - 2008 Inventions

2000

Hybrid Car
- Toyota released the Toyota Prius, the first hybrid four-door sedan available in the United States. Hybrid cars use a gasoline or diesel engine to power a motor. When the power of the motor is not required to move the vehicle, the motor can shut off, saving energy, or can be used to generate electricity that is stored in batteries, and later used to power the car. Between 2004 and 2009 it is estimated that 1.25 million of these vehicles were sold in the United

States. To this day the Prius is still the most popular vehicle of its kind.

2001

Segway PT
- Created by Dean Kamen the Segway Human Transporter is the first self-balancing, electric-powered transportation machine. It is a personal transport device that uses five gyroscopes and a built-in computer to remain upright.

iPod 1st Generation
- On October 23, 2001 Apple Computers publicly announced their portable music digital player, the iPod, created under project codename Dulcimer. One man that could be named the father of the iPod is Tony Fadell. Tony, a former employee of General Magic and Phillips, wanted to invent a better MP3 player. He went to work for Apple Computers in 2001 as an independent contractor, leading a team of thirty people to develop the new MP3 player. Within eight months, Tony Fadell's team and PortalPlayer completed a prototype iPod and Apple polished the user interface adding the famous scroll wheel.

Inventions & Events

- Apple announced in April 2007 that the 100 millionth iPod had been sold. Apple claims the iPod is the fastest-selling music player in history. It is estimated that approximately 86% of MP3 player users own an iPod, an astounding figure.

2002

Camera Phones

- Introduced to the North American marketplace in 2002, an estimated 80 million camera phones were sold in 2003, — 6 million in the U.S. alone. By 2003 more camera phones were sold worldwide than stand-alone digital cameras. At the end of 2008, the world-installed base of camera phones was 1.9 billion.

2003

Itunes Music Store

- The concept was simple: sell songs in digital format for less than a buck and let buyers play them whenever and wherever they like—as long as it was on an Apple iPod. Steve Jobs, Apple's CEO spent the previous year negotiating an unprecedented deal with all five major music labels and thousands of independents. His iTunes software, would become a gateway to the Music Store, where you could easily find and save music to your hard drive, CD or iPod music player—no subscription necessary, just 99 cents per song, or $9.99 for an album. As of January 2009, the store has sold 6 billion songs, accounting for 70% of worldwide online digital music sales and making the service the largest legal music retailer.

2004

DirecTV HD DVR
- Rated by CNET as one of the top ten products at the CES 2004 show, this TIVO device took digital video recording to the next level. The 250GB drive held 30 hours of high-def programming or 200 hours of standard TV. I bought one of these puppies when they first arrived in the marketplace and it was one of the best a/v component purchases I have ever made.

2005

YouTube
- Created in February 2005, by three former PayPal employees, YouTube was touted as a cutting-edge video sharing service. In November 2006, YouTube, LLC was bought by Google Inc. for $1.65 billion, and is now operat-

ed as a subsidiary of Google. Alexa ranks YouTube as the fourth most visited website on the Internet, behind Google, Yahoo! and Facebook.

2006
Wii

- Wii is a home video game console released by Nintendo. A distinguishing feature of the console is its wireless controller, the Wii Remote, which can be used as a handheld pointing device and detects movement in three dimensions. Another distinctive feature of the console is WiiConnect24, which enables it to receive messages and updates over the Internet while in standby mode. As of December 2009, the Wii leads the generation over the PlayStation 3 and Xbox 360 in worldwide sales.

2007

The iPhone

- Who else, but of course Steve Jobs, CEO for Apple, Inc. to take smartphones to a higher standard. This device, though controversial, is pretty, touchy-feely, and has a tremendous future. Approximately 6.4 million iPhones are active in the U.S. alone. 33.75 milliion of the devices have been sold world-wide to date.

2008

Amazon Kindle

- With the paper-like legibility of electronic ink, long battery life, and the ability to hold thousands of pages, e-book readers were already quite handy in 2008. But Amazon made them even more convenient by adding a free cellular connection for plucking newspapers, magazines—even entire books—out of the air in seconds. A truly brilliant innovation!

2000 - 2008 Events

2000

The dot-com bubble bursts
- The dot-com bubble (also referred to as the dot-com boom, the Internet bubble and the information technology bubble)[1] was a historic speculative bubble covering roughly 1997–2000 (with a climax on March 10, 2000, with the NASDAQ peaking at 5,408.60[2] in intraday trading before closing at 5,048.62) during which stock markets in industrialized nations saw their equity value rise rapidly from growth in the Internet sector and related fields. While the latter part was a boom and bust cycle, the Internet boom is sometimes meant to refer to the steady commercial growth of the Internet with the advent of the World Wide Web, as exemplified by the first release of the Mosaic web browser in 1993, and continuing through the 1990s.

Vladimir Putin is elected president of Russia
- Presidential elections were held in Russia on 26 March 2000.[1] Incumbent Prime Minister and acting President Vladimir Putin, who had succeeded Boris Yeltsin on his resignation on 31 December 1999, was seeking a four-year

term in his own right and won the elections in the first round.

Concorde crashes in France, killing 113

- July 25, an Air France Concorde jetliner en route to New York slammed into a hotel outside Paris today shortly after takeoff, killing all 109 people aboard and four more people on the ground.
- The charter flight burst into flames on impact in the first-ever crash of the needle-nosed supersonic jet. The passengers, mostly German tourists, were headed to New York to catch a luxury cruise to South America.
- Air France said there were 100 passengers aboard, including an American, and nine crew members. State Department sources identified the American as Christopher Behrens, an Air France retiree living in Germany. The passenger list also included 96 Germans, two Danes and an Austrian.

Personal home computers break the 1GHz barrier

- AMD's launch partners, Compaq Computer and Gateway, will get first dibs on the speedy new processors, Steve Lapinski, director of product marketing at AMD's Computation Products Group, said in a conference call with media and analysts today. The chip maker is scheduled to start volume shipments of the 1GHz Athlons to other PC vendors and the general market first in April, he added.

Sydney hosts the Olympic Games
- The Sydney 2000 Summer Olympic Games or the Millennium Olympic Games/Games of the New Millennium, officially known as the Games of the XXVII Olympiad, were an international multi-sport event which was celebrated between 15 September and 1 October 2000 in Sydney, New South Wales, Australia. It was the second time that the Summer Olympics were held in the Southern Hemisphere, the first one being in Melbourne, Victoria in 1956.

2001

George Bush is sworn in as the 43rd President of the USA
- The first inauguration of George W. Bush as the 43rd President of the United States of America took place on January 20, 2001. The inauguration marked the commencement of the first four-year term of George W. Bush as President and Dick Cheney as Vice President. Chief Justice William Rehnquist administered the oath

of office at 12:01 p.m.[1] An estimated 300,000 people attended the swearing-in ceremony.[

Space station Mir is deorbited

- The deorbit of Mir was the controlled atmospheric re-entry of the modular Russian space station Mir carried out on March 23, 2001. Major components ranged from about 5 to 15 years in age, and included the Mir Core Module, Kvant-1, Kvant-2, Kristall, Spektr, Priroda, and Docking Module. Although Russia was optimistic about Mir's future, the country's commitments to the International Space Station project left no funding to support Mir.[1]
- The deorbit was carried out in three stages. The first stage was waiting for atmospheric drag to decay the orbit an average of 220 kilometers (137 mi). This began with the docking of Progress M1-5. The second stage was the transfer of the station into a 165 × 220 km (103 × 137 mi) orbit. This was achieved with two burns of the Progress M1-5's control engines at 00:32 UTC and 02:01 UTC on March 23, 2001. After a two-orbit pause, the third and final stage of Mir's deorbit began with the firing of Progress M1-5's control engines and main engine at 05:08 UTC, lasting a little over 22 minutes. The atmospheric re-entry at the altitude of 100 kilo-

metres (62 mi) occurred at 05:44 UTC near Nadi, Fiji.

The world's first space tourist
- April 28, an American businessman Dennis Tito became history's first space tourist, paying his own way to the International Space Station aboard a Russian Soyuz spacecraft. Forty years to the month after Yuri Gagarin became the first person in space, Tito showed that there was money to be made in human spaceflight -- potentially lots of money, as he plunked down a reported $20 million for his flight.

A devastating terrorist attack leaves 3,000 dead in America
- On September 11, 2001, at 8:45 a.m. on a clear Tuesday morning, an American Airlines Boeing 767 loaded with 20,000 gallons of jet fuel crashed into the north tower of the World Trade Center in New York City. The impact left a gaping, burning hole near the 80th floor of the 110-story skyscraper, instantly killing hundreds of people and trapping hundreds more in higher floors. As the evacuation of the tower and its twin got underway, television cameras broadcasted live images of what initially appeared to be a freak accident. Then, 18 minutes after the first plane hit, a second Boeing 767–United Air-

lines Flight 175–appeared out of the sky, turned sharply toward the World Trade Center and sliced into the south tower near the 60th floor. The collision caused a massive explosion that showered burning debris over surrounding buildings and the streets below. America was under attack.
- September 11, 2001, was the deadliest day in history for New York City firefighters: 343 were killed.
- The attackers were Islamic terrorists from Saudi Arabia and several other Arab nations. Reportedly financed by Saudi fugitive Osama bin Laden's al-Qaeda terrorist organization, they were allegedly acting in retaliation for America's support of Israel, its involvement in the Persian Gulf War and its continued military presence in the Middle East. Some of the terrorists had lived in the United States for more than a year and had taken flying lessons at American commercial flight schools. Others had slipped into the country in the months before September 11 and acted as the "muscle" in the operation. The 19 terrorists easily smuggled box-cutters and knives through security at three East Coast airports and boarded four flights bound for California, chosen because the planes were loaded with fuel for the long transcontinental journey. Soon after takeoff, the terrorists commandeered

the four planes and took the controls, transforming ordinary commuter jets into guided missiles.
- As millions watched the events unfolding in New York, American Airlines Flight 77 circled over downtown Washington, D.C., and slammed into the west side of the Pentagon military headquarters at 9:45 a.m. Jet fuel from the Boeing 757 caused a devastating inferno that led to the structural collapse of a portion of the giant concrete building. All told, 125 military personnel and civilians were killed in the Pentagon, along with all 64 people aboard the airliner.
- Less than 15 minutes after the terrorists struck the nerve center of the U.S. military, the horror in New York took a catastrophic turn for the worse when the south tower of the World Trade Center collapsed in a massive cloud of dust and smoke. The structural steel of the skyscraper, built to withstand winds in excess of 200 miles per hour and a large conventional fire, could not withstand the tremendous heat generated by the burning jet fuel. At 10:30 a.m., the other Trade Center tower collapsed. Close to 3,000 people died in the World Trade Center and its vicinity, including a staggering 343 firefighters and paramedics, 23 New York City police officers and 37 Port Authority police officers who were struggling to complete an evacuation of the buildings and save the office workers

trapped on higher floors. Only six people in the World Trade Center towers at the time of their collapse survived. Almost 10,000 others were treated for injuries, many severe.
- Meanwhile, a fourth California-bound plane– United Flight 93–was hijacked about 40 minutes after leaving Newark International Airport in New Jersey. Because the plane had been delayed in taking off, passengers on board learned of events in New York and Washington via cell phone and Airfone calls to the ground. Knowing that the aircraft was not returning to an airport as the hijackers claimed, a group of passengers and flight attendants planned an insurrection. One of the passengers, Thomas Burnett Jr., told his wife over the phone that "I know we're all going to die. There's three of us who are going to do something about it. I love you, honey." Another passenger–Todd Beamer–was heard saying "Are you guys ready? Let's roll" over an open line. Sandy Bradshaw, a flight attendant, called her husband and explained that she had slipped into a galley and was filling pitchers with boiling water. Her last words to him were "Everyone's running to first class. I've got to go. Bye."
- The passengers fought the four hijackers and are suspected to have attacked the cockpit with a fire extinguisher. The plane then flipped over

and sped toward the ground at upwards of 500 miles per hour, crashing in a rural field in western Pennsylvania at 10:10 a.m. All 45 people aboard were killed. Its intended target is not known, but theories include the White House, the U.S. Capitol, the Camp David presidential retreat in Maryland or one of several nuclear power plants along the eastern seaboard.
- At 7 p.m., President George W. Bush, who had spent the day being shuttled around the country because of security concerns, returned to the White House. At 9 p.m., he delivered a televised address from the Oval Office, declaring, "Terrorist attacks can shake the foundations of our biggest buildings, but they cannot touch the foundation of America. These acts shatter steel, but they cannot dent the steel of American resolve." In a reference to the eventual U.S. military response he declared, "We will make no distinction between the terrorists who committed these acts and those who harbor them."

Apple launches the iPod
- CUPERTINO, California—October 23, 2001—Apple® today introduced iPod™, a breakthrough MP3 music player that packs up to 1,000 CD-quality songs into an ultra-portable, 6.5 ounce design that fits in your pocket. iPod combines a major advance in portable music

device design with Apple's legendary ease of use and Auto-Sync, which automatically downloads all your iTunes™ songs and playlists into your iPod, and keeps them up to date whenever you plug your iPod into your Mac®.

2002

Apple introduces the iMac G4
- The iMac G4 is an all-in-one desktop computer produced and sold by Apple Inc. from 2002 to mid-2004, succeeding the egg-shaped iMac G3 and being succeeded by the iMac G5.

The deadliest act of terrorism in the history of Indonesia
- 12 October 2002 — The coordinated bomb attacks occurred on in the tourist district of Kuta, Bali. The attack was claimed as the deadliest act of terrorism in the history of Indonesia according to the current police general, killing 202 people, (including 88 Australians, and 38 Indonesian citizens).[7] A further 240 people were injured. Various members of Jemaah Islamiyah, a violent Islamist group, were convicted in relation to the bombings, including three individuals who were sentenced to death.

2003

Space Shuttle Columbia disaster
- On Feb. 1, 2003, space shuttle Columbia broke up as it returned to Earth, killing the seven astronauts on board. NASA suspended space shuttle flights for more than two years as it investigated the disaster.
- An investigation board determined that a large piece of foam fell from the shuttle's external tank and fatally breached the spacecraft wing. This problem with foam had been known for years, and NASA came under intense scrutiny in Congress and in the media for allowing the situation to continue.

The invasion of Iraq
- The 2003 invasion of Iraq lasted from 19 March – 1 May 2003 and signaled the start of the conflict that later came to be known as the Iraq War, which was dubbed Operation Iraqi Freedom by the United States (prior to 19 March, the mission in Iraq was called Operation Enduring Freedom, a carryover from the conflict in Afghanistan[19]). The invasion consisted of 21 days of major combat operations, in which a combined force of troops from the United States, the United Kingdom, Australia, Poland

and Spain invaded Iraq and deposed the Ba'athist government of Saddam Hussein. The invasion phase consisted primarily of a conventionally fought war which concluded with the capture of the Iraqi capital of Baghdad by American forces.
- Four countries participated with troops during the initial invasion phase, which lasted from 19 March to 9 April 2003. These were the United States (148,000), United Kingdom (45,000), Australia (2,000), and Poland (194). 36 other countries were involved in its aftermath. In preparation for the invasion, 100,000 U.S. troops were assembled in Kuwait by 18 February.[20] The coalition forces also received support from Kurdish irregulars in Iraqi Kurdistan.

Record heat waves kill tens of thousands in Europe

- October 9, 2003 (ENS) - A record heat wave scorched Europe in August 2003, claiming an estimated 35,000 lives. In France alone, 14,802 people died from the searing temperatures - more than 19 times the death toll from the SARS epidemic worldwide. In the worst heat spell in decades, temperatures in France soared to 104 degrees Fahrenheit (40 degrees Celsius) and remained unusually high for two weeks.

MySpace is launched
- Myspace was founded in 2003 by Chris DeWolfe and Tom Anderson, and was later acquired by News Corporation in July 2005 for $580 million. From 2005 until early 2008, Myspace was the most visited social networking site in the world, and in June 2006 surpassed Google as the most visited website in the United States. In April 2008, Myspace was overtaken by Facebook in the number of unique worldwide visitors, and was surpassed in the number of unique U.S. visitors in May 2009, though Myspace generated $800 million in revenue during the 2008 fiscal year. Since then, the number of Myspace users has declined steadily in spite of several redesigns. As of May 2014, Myspace was ranked 982 by total web traffic, and 392 in the United States.[

China launches its first manned space mission
- Oct 16, 2003, China completed its first manned space flight Thursday when the Shenzhou V capsule with astronaut Yang Liwei returned safely to Earth, sparking celebrations and a pledge of a new mission within two years.

2004

The first recorded hurricane in the South Atlantic
- U.S. officials said the storm, which struck land some 520 miles southwest of Rio de Janeiro packing sustained winds of more than 74 mph, appeared to be the first hurricane on record in the South Atlantic.

George W. Bush is re-elected
- The United States presidential election of 2004 was the 55th quadrennial presidential election. It was held on Tuesday, November 2, 2004. Republican Party candidate and incumbent President George W. Bush defeated Democratic Party candidate John Kerry, the then-junior Senator from Massachusetts.
- Bush, along with incumbent Vice President Dick Cheney, were renominated by their party with little difficulty. Howard Dean was initially the frontrunner for the Democratic Party's nomination, but Kerry won nearly all of the primaries and caucuses. Kerry chose another candidate, Senator John Edwards of North Carolina, to be his running mate.

Athens hosts the Olympic Games
- The 2004 Summer Olympic Games, officially known as the Games of the XXVIII Olympiad, was a premier international multi-sport event held in Athens, Greece, from 13 to 29 August 2004 with the motto Welcome Home. 10,625 athletes competed, some 600 more than expected, accompanied by 5,501 team officials from 201 countries. There were 301 medal events in 28 different sports. Athens 2004 marked the first time since the 1996 Summer Olympics that all countries with a National Olympic Committee were in attendance. It was also the first time since 1896 (other than the since-downgraded 1906 Intercalated Games) that the Olympics were held in Greece.

Train bombings in Madrid kill nearly 200 people
- On March 12, in the most devastating terrorist attack in Spanish history, 10 bombs detonating minutes apart ripped through crowded commuter trains at three Madrid stations early Thursday, killing nearly 200 people, injuring 1,400 and sending this capital into convulsions of shock and horror three days before a national election.

Hubble Ultra Deep Field

- The Hubble Ultra-Deep Field (HUDF) is an image of a small region of space in the constellation Fornax, composited from Hubble Space Telescope data accumulated over a period from September 24, 2003, through to January 16, 2004. Looking back approximately 13 billion years (between 400 and 800 million years after the Big Bang) it will be used to search for galaxies that existed at that time. The HUDF image was taken in a section of the sky with a low density of bright stars in the near-field, allowing much better viewing of dimmer, more distant objects. The image contains an estimated 10,000 galaxies. In August and September 2009, the Hubble's Deep Field was expanded using the infrared channel of the recently attached Wide Field Camera 3 (WFC3). When combined with existing HUDF data, astronomers were able to identify a new list of potentially very distant galaxies.

Mars Exploration Rovers

- NASA's twin robot geologists, the Mars Exploration Rovers, launched toward Mars on June 10 and July 7, 2003, in search of answers about the history of water on Mars. They landed on Mars January 3 and January 24 PST, 2004 (January 4 and January 25 UTC, 2004).

The first privately funded human spaceflight

- SpaceShipOne is a suborbital air-launched spaceplane that completed the first manned private spaceflight in 2004. That same year, it won the US$10 million Ansari X Prize and was immediately retired from active service. Its mother ship was named "White Knight". Both craft were developed and flown by Mojave Aerospace Ventures, which was a joint venture between Paul Allen and Scaled Composites, Burt Rutan's aviation company. Allen provided the funding of approximately US$25 million.

Facebook is launched

- Facebook is a social networking service launched in February 2004, owned and operated by Facebook. It was founded by Mark Zuckerberg with his college roommates and fellow Harvard University students Eduardo Saverin, Andrew McCollum, Dustin Moskovitz and Chris Hughes. The website's membership was initially limited by the founders to Harvard students, but was expanded to other colleges in the Boston area, the Ivy League, and gradually most universities in Canada and the United States, corporations, and by September 2006, to everyone of age 13 and older to make a group with a valid email address.

World's first 1 gigabyte SD card

- January 27, 2004 – SanDisk Corporation is shipping the world's first production one-gigabyte (GB) Secure Digital (SD) flash card, which contains a unique "stackable" packaging technology jointly implemented with Sharp Corporation of Japan. This new package employs a low-cost, high-yielding die-stacking process that is designed to enable SanDisk to double the memory capacity without increasing the size of the card, thus launching a new generation of competitively-priced, higher-density flash devices that can store unprecedented amounts of pictures, music and video.

London's skyline gets a new landmark

- The Shard is the highly visible landmark at the heart of London Bridge Quarter, a 2m sq ft gross mixed-use development which, once complete, will create more than 12,000 jobs. London Bridge Quarter is a key part of the regeneration of this part of London and benefits from access to one of London's key transport hubs, London Bridge Station. The development has transformed London Bridge Station delivering a new bus station and train station concourse, and this will be linked by a central plaza which will open in 2013. This plaza will also link The Shard to its' sister building The Place, a new 17 storey HQ building due to complete in Spring 2013.

Indian Ocean earthquake leaves a quarter of a million dead
- The death toll from last month's Indian Ocean tsunami disaster rose towards a quarter of a million Wednesday while floods hampered relief efforts in worst-hit Indonesia's Aceh province.
- The Indonesian death toll jumped to 166,320, the health ministry said late Wednesday, more than 50,000 higher than the government's previous tally.
- A member of the ministry's disaster centre, Dr. Ina, told AFP that 166,080 people had been confirmed killed in Aceh, while there were 240 fatalities in the neighboring province of North Sumatra.
- With the latest tolls, the tsunamis triggered by a 9.0-magnitude quake off the coast of Sumatra island have left nearly 220,000 dead in 11 Indian Ocean countries.

2005

YouTube is launched
- Three former PayPal employees created YouTube in February 2005. In November 2006,

YouTube, LLC was bought by Google Inc. for $1.65 billion, and is now operated as a subsidiary of Google.

USB flash drives replace floppy disks
- A USB flash drive is a data storage device that includes flash memory with an integrated Universal Serial Bus (USB) interface. USB flash drives are typically removable and rewritable, and physically much smaller than an optical disc.

Suicide bombers in London kill 56 people, injure 700 others
- On the morning of Thursday, 7 July 2005, four Islamist men detonated four bombs—three in quick succession aboard London Underground trains across the city and, later, a fourth on a double-decker bus in Tavistock Square. As well as the four bombers, 52 civilians were killed and over 700 more were injured in the attacks, the United Kingdom's worst terrorist incident since the 1988 Lockerbie bombing as well as the country's first ever suicide attack.

Hurricane Katrina floods New Orleans
- On August 31, The New Orleans Times-Picayune reported on its Web site Tuesday that floodwaters rushed into the streets when canal

levees on opposite sides of the city ruptured. Louisiana governor Kathleen Blanco responded by ordering everyone out of New Orleans.
- Dozens of deaths across the Gulf Coast already have been attributed to Hurricane Katrina. Authorities fear flooding in New Orleans could increase the toll and create a potentially serious public health problem.

Angela Merkel becomes the first female Chancellor of Germany
- Germany was on the brink of a new and volatile political era, after a deal was agreed that will see the conservative leader Angela Merkel become the country's first ever woman chancellor.
- Three weeks of wrangling over an indecisive election ended when the chancellor, Gerhard Schröder, announced he was resigning. Mrs Merkel will now become chancellor and lead a "grand coalition" between her Christian Democrat party and its Bavarian ally the Christian Social Union, and Mr Schröder's Social Democrats.

2006

Twitter is launched
- Twitter was created in March 2006 by Jack Dorsey, Evan Williams, Biz Stone and Noah Glass and by July 2006, the site was launched. The service rapidly gained worldwide popularity, with 500 million registered users in 2012, who posted 340 million tweets per day.

North Korea conducts its first nuclear test
- Monday, Oct. 9 — North Korea said Sunday night that it had set off its first nuclear test, becoming the eighth country in history, and arguably the most unstable and most dangerous, to proclaim that it has joined the club of nuclear weapons states.

Saddam Hussein is executed
- The execution of Saddam Hussein took place on Saturday 30 December 2006. Hussein was sentenced to death by hanging, after being found guilty and convicted of crimes against humanity by the Iraqi Special Tribunal for the murder of 148 Iraqi Shi'ite in the town of Dujail in 1982, in retaliation for an assassination attempt against him.

2007

Global economic downturn
- The financial crisis of 2007–2008, also known as the Global Financial Crisis and 2008 financial crisis, is considered by many economists the worst financial crisis since the Great Depression of the 1930s.[1] It resulted in the threat of total collapse of large financial institutions, the bailout of banks by national governments, and downturns in stock markets around the world. In many areas, the housing market also suffered, resulting in evictions, foreclosures and prolonged unemployment.

Nicolas Sarkozy is elected President of the French Republic
- The 2007 French presidential election, the ninth of the Fifth French Republic was held to elect the successor to Jacques Chirac as president of France for a five-year term.
- The winner, decided on 5 and 6 May 2007, was Nicolas Sarkozy. The first round of voting took place on Saturday, 21 April 2007 (French territories in the Americas and the Eastern Pacific) and Sunday, 22 April 2007 (French territories in the Western Pacific, Indian Ocean, and Metropolitan France). As no candidate obtained a

majority (50 percent plus one), a second round between the two leading candidates, Nicolas Sarkozy and Ségolène Royal, took place on Saturday, 5 May and Sunday, 6 May 2007.
- Sarkozy and Royal both represented a generational change. Either candidate would have become the first French president to be born after World War II,[1] the first to have seen adulthood under the Fifth Republic and the first not to have been in politics under Charles de Gaulle.

Brown succeeds Blair as Prime Minister of Great Britain

- Tony Blair was 44, making him the youngest British prime minister since Lord Liverpool in 1812. (Blair was often compared with the sitting U.S. president, Bill Clinton, who was 46 when he took office in 1993.) Blair was re-elected in Parliamentary elections in 2001 and 2005. He stepped down as the prime minister on 27 June 2007 and was succeeded by the Chancellor of the Exchequer, Gordon Brown.

Apple debuts the iPhone

- January 9, 2007, Apple Inc. CEO Steve Jobs unveils the iPhone—a touchscreen mobile phone with an iPod, camera and Web-browsing capabilities, among other features—at the Macworld convention in San Francisco. Jobs, dressed in his customary jeans and black mock turtleneck, called the iPhone a "revolutionary and magical product that is literally five years ahead of any other mobile phone." When it went on sale in the United States six months later, on June 29, amidst huge hype, thousands of customers lined up at Apple stores across the country to be among the first to purchase an iPhone.

Multiple suicide bombings kill 796 people in Kahtaniya, northern Iraq

- The Yazidi communities bombings occurred at 8pm local time on 14th August 2007, when four co-ordinated suicide bomb attacks detonated in the villages of Kahtaniya and Jazeera, near Mosul. Entire neighbourhoods were flattened by the blasts. Iraqi Red Crescent's estimates stated that 796 were killed and 1,562 wounded, making it the Iraq War's most deadly car bomb attack during the period of American combat operations. It was also the second deadliest act of terrorism in the world – following only behind the 9/11 attacks on the U.S. which killed 3,000 people. No group claimed responsibility for the attack, though Al-Qaeda were suspected.

Amazon releases the Kindle

- The Amazon Kindle is a series of e-book readers designed and marketed by Amazon.com. Amazon Kindle devices enable users to shop for, download, browse, and read e-books, newspapers, magazines, blogs, and other digital media via wireless networking. The hardware platform, developed by Amazon.com subsidiary Lab126, began as a single device and now comprises a range of devices, including dedicated e-readers with E Ink electronic paper displays, and Android-based tablets with color LCD screens.Google Street View is launched

Benazir Bhutto is assassinated in Pakistan

- The assassination of Benazir Bhutto occurred on 27 December 2007 in Rawalpindi, Pakistan. Bhutto, twice Prime Minister of Pakistan (1988–1990; 1993–1996) and then-leader of the opposition Pakistan Peoples Party, had been campaigning ahead of elections scheduled for January 2008. Shots were fired at her after a political rally at Liaquat National Bagh, and a suicide bomb was detonated immediately following the shooting.

2008

Cyclone Nargis devastates Burma
- With the death toll approaching 10,000 from the devastating cyclone that slammed Myanmar on Saturday, U.N. agencies and independent humanitarian groups rushed to prepare assistance for victims.

Oil prices hit a record high
- Oil prices jumped $5 to a record high above $147 a barrel on Friday amid growing worries about threats to supplies from Iran and Nigeria and a strike by Brazilian oil workers next week.

The Internet continues to boom
- The final quarter of 2013 proved to be the most successful quarter of the year for .com and .net.
- VeriSign's latest domain name industry brief revealed that 127.2 million domain names were registered in .com and .net in Q4 2013. This represented a 5 percent increase on the previous year, with .com attracting 112 million new registration and .net attracting 15.2 million.
- Just over 270 million domain names were registered across all TLDs in Q4 2013, according to VeriSign, representing an increase of five million

domain names, or 1.9 percent over the previous quarter.

Scientists extract images directly from the brain

- Researchers from Japan's ATR Computational Neuroscience Laboratories have developed new brain analysis technology that can reconstruct the images inside a person's mind and display them on a computer monitor, it was announced on December 11. According to the researchers, further development of the technology may soon make it possible to view other people's dreams while they sleep.

Beijing hosts the Olympic games

- To be held between the 8th and 24th August, 2008 there will be 28 major and 302 minor competitive events in which athletes from all over the world in 37 venues will participate. Among all the venues, 31 are in Beijing and six in Hong Kong, Qingdao, Qinhuangdao, Shanghai, Shenyang and Tianjin.

THE END

I consider 2008 as the last year that the USA prospered. Actually that year was also the beginning of the largest down-turn since 1929. Not only were we in trouble, but the entire world seemed to be in trouble. Stock markets were going down and the prognosis was grim.

Then along came BO and his promise of "Hope & Change". That didn't work as of the printing of this book (2014). He even received a second term to "complete his promise" and it's not working - but then again, neither is half of the population.

I gathered the information in this book for the express purpose of showing our "younger generations" that America was an exciting place to live at one time. There was already "Hope & Change" for the good and it is clearly evident that the USA was the place to be.

Yes - we lived through wars and downturns, but we held our heads high and persevered. We had faith in the very fiber of our nation that better times were ahead. We prospered and rose to great heights that can be realized and appreciated to this day.

It has been said that every country only has a lifetime of about 250 years before changes happen. We are now at 238. Are we due for change?

Certainly, BO's "change" is not what our fore-fathers would have had in mind. Neither will our modern-day patriots confess to this idea. We were brought up in FREEDOM believing in the Constitution and Bill of Rights. NO ONE should take that away without a fight. If you don't want to fight for your rights, you'll deserve what is handed to you by the government. If it is more honorable for you to receive something you haven't worked for then you are among the "suckers" that are bleeding the country dry.

I can only pray that my children, grandchildren & great-grandchildren read and understand that this country was founded on faith, guts and glory that far out-shown any other country in the modern world. And - for 230+ years we have excelled in displaying to the world our expertise and compassion that is truly lacking today.

May God grant us a revival.

Just remember kids - your parents and Grandparents made it through school without Google

Truly THE END

www.ingramcontent.com/pod-product-compliance
Lightning Source LLC
Chambersburg PA
CBHW061424040426
42450CB00007B/889